WORDS OF PRAISE

for the authors of

THINK OUT OF THE BOX

"We couldn't have accomplished what we did at Apple Computer without Mike Vance."

> —*A.C. (Mike) Markkula,*
> *Chairman, Apple Computer*

"Through Diane's and Mike's help, we developed a training program that allowed one of our companies to become a leader."

> — *Tom Guest, Manager of Market*
> *Development, Johnson & Johnson*

"My career can be neatly divided between the time before I used Vance's ideas to help me 'think out of the box'— when not much happened—and the time after I began to put his ideas to work—when everything I ever wanted to achieve came true."

> —*Morely Winograd, Western Region Sales*
> *Vice-President, AT&T Small Business Markets*

"In over 10 years of working with Mike Vance and Diane Deacon, I have consistently found their concepts drive action."

> —*Jon Lee, Director, Corporate Medical*
> *Services, Owens Corning Fiberglas*

THINK

OUT OF THE

BOX

THINK

OUT OF THE

BOX

By
Mike Vance and Diane Deacon

Career Press
3 Tice Road
P.O. Box 687
Franklin Lakes, NJ 07417
800-CAREER-1
201-848-0310 (NJ and outside U.S.)
FAX: 201-848-1727

THINK OUT OF THE BOX (PAPERBACK)
Cover design by Ad/Art Studios
Printed in the U.S.A. by Book-mart Press

To order this title, please call toll-free 1-800-CAREER-1 (NJ and Canada: 201-848-0310) to order using VISA or MasterCard, or for further information on books from Career Press.

Library of Congress Cataloging-in-Publication Data

Vance, Mike.
    Think out of the box / by Mike Vance and Diane Deacon.
        p.   cm.
    Includes index.
    ISBN 1-56414-186-1
    1. Creative ability in business. 2. Organizational change.
3. Corporate culture. 4. Success in business.   I. Deacon, Diane,
1960-   . II. Title.
HD53.V354 1995
658.4'06—dc20   95-24876
                                                                   CIP

This book and the concepts, ideas and techniques contained on its pages are dedicated to the following people who inspired them:

Walt Disney and his brother Roy O. Disney. They thought out of the box to create the Disney dream.

E. Cardon Walker and Michael Eisner. Their thinking out of the box kept the dream alive and growing.

Jack Welch and A.C. (Mike) Markkula. They thought out of the bureaucracy box to inspire a new leadership style at General Electric and Apple Computer.

ACKNOWLEDGMENTS

The literary achievements and life examples of Jim and Ellie Newton and Danny and Theo Cox stimulated us to take up the pen and leave something behind. John Hoover worked the original manuscript, translating our thoughts and feelings on many subjects to the page. Betsy Sheldon, our editor, helped polish and refine and made the book come together. She is a real pro. Ralph and Virginia Vance, my mother and father, presented me with a lifetime of exemplary values and love. Mark, John and Vanessa Vance—as well as all the other members of my family—have been showing me their love since birth.

Diane and I also want to thank some good friends: Steve and Ruth Pfaff, Don and Nancy Wilder, George and Sherry Fink, Merritt Fink, Jon Lee, Larry and Robbie Broedow, Ed and Chris Craig, Val Halamandaris and his brother Bill. We also extend our gratitude to the thousands of individuals who have acted on the ideas we've planted in their minds and to the companies that have implemented many of the ideas and techniques presented in this book.

—Mike Vance

My deepest gratitude goes to Mike Vance, my partner and friend, who has mentored me throughout the years and taught me how to think new thoughts.

This book is also dedicated to Larry and Shirley Deacon, my parents, who have been both teachers and friends to me, and to all the members of my family and dear friends who have given me the foundation for entrepreneurship.

—Diane Deacon

CONTENTS

PROLOGUE

Two imposing bodyguards dressed in stylish dark blue suits took their positions beside each entry door at the back of the large hotel ballroom. They were accompanying Louis Lundborg, the powerful chairman of the Bank of America. Lundborg had come to hear Mike Vance present the opening address at the Apple Computer convention near San Francisco.

Lundborg walked down the center aisle, through throngs of people, to a seat reserved for him in the front row. He was a handsome, distinguished and urbane gentleman. He looked exactly like you would expect the Bank of America chairman to look: imposing. The rest of the audience was a different story. The burgeoning computer industry was not known for its conservative dress.

Mike and Louis were old friends. Lundborg had appeared on Mike's 1960s Los Angeles television show "Men at the Top," and participated in a number of Mike's organizational development (OD) programs at The Walt Disney Company. The strong bond between them was grounded by Lundborg's sage counsel and advice over the years. Mike smiled at Louis. Lundborg gave Mike a thumbs-up sign.

Mike composed his thoughts as hundreds of Apple Computer family members took their seats and awaited the beginning of the gathering. There were dealers, distributors, suppliers, programmers, journalists, the company's founders, investors, friends and true believers. The crowd was expectant, buzzing with excitement in anticipation of a long-awaited new product introduction and the appearance of Steve Jobs later that day.

As he waited near the stage, Mike carefully studied the individuals entering the room, most of whom he knew well. Surveying the faces of the audience before a presentation is a ritual with Mike, who thinks of this practice as looking into the eyes and soul of his audience. As he prepared to address the Apple audience, Mike could see the excitement in the eyes of the crowd.

The young company was riding high. Apple was at its zenith. It was the darling of Wall Street and business magazine covers, reaffirming the vitality of entrepreneurial spirit in America. Mike was about to speak for three hours on the "challenging task" of building a billion-dollar company from scratch in a few years. Apple had asked Mike to talk about the creative principles behind "thinking out of the box," concluding with some personal stories about Jobs to reveal the nature of his inquisitive mind and inspirational qualities.

Mike knew countless critics had already written volumes about Steve's caustic verbal explosions. But Mike knew another side of Jobs' temperament that balanced out the picture—the deeply personal, human side that exposed a warm, vulnerable and concerned person beneath the sometimes studied veneer.

The meeting was called to order and Mike was introduced. He told the audience about the tribulations of success that were staring them in the face. He cautioned them that the biggest challenges of all were to live with their success, remain proud, continue to learn, avoid arrogance and continually create new solutions. He quoted Apple cofounder, A.C. (Mike) Markkula:

"The most important asset we have is a good set of values. We believe 'management by values' is the only way to go."

Mike challenged the Apple family to continue uncovering the secrets of highly creative people, to maintain their curiosity, openness and willingness to try new ideas. He reminded them of how heated debates had produced a better team, a better company and a better product.

Mike, who has worked with too many companies who pay lip service to the concept of upholding higher values, complimented the people at Apple for upholding such values and standards. He also forewarned them of the temptation among growing companies to become bureaucratic and political. Bureaucracies and politics, he cautioned, cause people to position themselves along party lines rather than stay loyal to the company's mission.

Mike reminded the Apple audience that they were an unruly bunch of rebels with a great cause—to revolutionize the way people work and live—and further challenged them to avoid petty thinking and elitism.

Mike concluded by attributing Apple's early success to its adherence to the essential elements of highly creative and innovative individuals and organizations. The following illustrations were on one of Mike's flip charts on the stage:

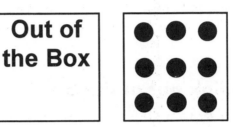

THINK Out of the Box

He explained that "think out of the box" is a metaphor for successful creative thinking. It employs the exercise of connecting nine dots laid out in the form of a box by using only four straight lines, without lifting your pen. The imaginary box contains the resources, tools, methods and techniques for opening the box, accomplished by connecting the dots through creative thinking. Each of the dots represent part of the formula for thinking out of the box.

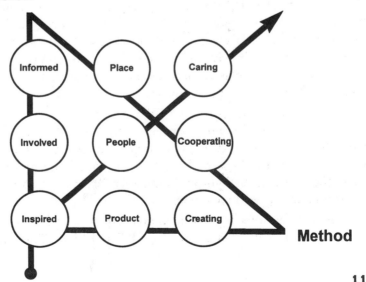

Competent and caring leadership that provides resource-rich environments will invariably produce the individual and organizational performance that business journalists and authors love to write about.

Much of what we say in the pages ahead may be controversial. But the principles and practices of highly creative people have been proven over time. The more we learn about them, the more timeless they become.

Why think out of the box?

The goal for every life form is, in part, to get out of the box. Birth itself is the preeminent example of getting outside the box. A chrysalis breaking open to reveal a butterfly, the earth bursting forth with the shoots of a new plant or an egg cracking at the persistent pecking of a chick are all examples of life struggling against the confines of environment.

Why think out of the box? To live. To be. To create. To renew.

Optimism is the fuel that fires creative thinking. We look outside the box, call upon our sense of vision, and imagine the best possible outcome. Kahlil Gibran observed, "Who would believe winter if winter said spring is in my heart?"

We also think out of the box to gain strategic advantage in our enterprises. The winds of change continue to blow at hurricane force in our expanding global village of transnational companies, where technology entrepreneurs are already surfing the Net. There is a surge of boundaryless culture and elusive organizational forms that baffle even the most erudite theoreticians of change.

Amid this tumult has emerged yet another buzzword for us to embrace like a long-awaited panacea. That ubiquitous word is "strategic." The goal of being strategic is to give us competitive advantage. It was this out-of-the-box thinking that produced the automobile, the train, the airplane, the light bulb, the Salk vaccine, elevators, air conditioners, plumbing and television.

The very latest technological innovations are called IAs—information appliances—instead of merely a PC, CP, TV or VCR. There are models that can fit into corners of your kitchen or hang from bathroom ceilings, and some can even be implanted into the walls.

IAs are the "brainchildren" of today's innovators. How about the brainchildren of the past? The innovators of the past created a product named "Wite-Out" to correct errors, "Post-it Notes" to stick little messages all over everything, and a really simple invention of brilliant engineering known as the paper clip. All of these brainchildren are from the out-of-the-box thinkers of yesterday. Who will be the parents of tomorrow's brainchildren? Where are they going to come from, these Edisons, Fermis, Disneys and Gateses?

Profiles in creativity

Models and experience are the best teachers because they make ideas real and measurable, rather than hypothetical. Between each of the nine chapters of this book, we profile an outstanding creative thinker—a superlative example who successfully illustrates the principles espoused in this book: Norman Brinker, Thomas Edison, Louis L'Amour, Frank Lloyd Wright, Dr. Vernon Luck, Buckminster Fuller, A.C. (Mike) Markkula, Jack Welch and Walt Disney. Nine profiles, nine out-of-the-box thinkers.

But our world will always need creative thinkers. After all, who will get cars off the ground by figuring out how they can hover rather than ride on wheels that require roads?

Where are you, Jules Verne?

Who will go beyond the outmoded, slow and costly form of transportation called an airplane by devising a way to let us soar on some kind of light beam?

Come back, Wilbur and Orville!

Who will help to eliminate microbes that consume us and shorten our time for dreaming, creating and living?

Revisit us, Madam Curie, and bring along Dr. Louis Pasteur.

Who will stop the pointless killing and endless warring by teaching us about how to love and how to have peace?

Speak to us again, Gandhi, Martin Luther King and Dr. Albert Schweitzer.

To think out of the box will become the catch phrase of the next millennium.

To think out of the box is the number-one challenge for enlightened persons.

To think out of the box requires that we are smart enough and sensitive enough to work on the needs our information age is generating.

The future is always challenging because it brings ever-increasing demands on our intellect and our resources.

The techniques presented in this book will assist you in meeting those challenges by going beyond conventional responses to higher creativity and innovative thinking.

CHAPTER 1

How did we get boxed in?

*The purpose of time is to provide a framework
so that everything doesn't happen at once.*

*The purpose of a box is to provide a
container for holding things inside.*

*We time travelers are continually trying
to think our way out of the box.*

Life is too long not to do it right. For most of us, there are approximately two and one half billion seconds between birth and death. That's a long period of time. Consider the number of experiences we can accumulate in two and a half billion seconds. And yet, we can't learn anything from experiences we're not having.

Some profound cosmological questions have haunted human beings from the start. Are we physical or spiritual? Some philosophers say we are essentially physical beings who have occasional spiritual experiences.

Other philosophers say we are primarily spiritual beings currently having physical experiences.

The spirits of certain people just seem to stick on us when we're with them. Their passions, their hopes, their dreams linger on in us, surfacing anew when something triggers our memory.

- Walt Disney was such a person.
- Roy Disney was such a person.
- Louis L'Amour was such a person.
- Thomas Edison was such a person.
- Dr. R. Buckminster Fuller was such a person.
- Frank Lloyd Wright was such a person.
- Dr. J. Vernon Luck was such a person.
- E. Cardon Walker is such a person.
- Jack Welch is such a person.
- Steve Jobs is such a person.
- Norman Brinker is such a person.
- A.C. (Mike) Markkula is such a person.

You'll meet each of these people and others in the pages ahead as we peel away layer after layer to gradually reveal the core of them from our point of view. We hope that you'll remember them and learn from them as we have. We hope part of them sticks to you as they have with us. They are out-of-the-box thinkers. We're certain each of them struggled, as we all must, to avoid being trapped in the unproductive box of pedestrian thinking. It's a constant challenge not to get boxed in.

We don't presume to have all the answers, but we continue to search for them. We don't expect you to agree with everything we've written here, but it is important to consider the concepts and attitudes we've observed that tend to box people in. Ideas that box us in are like sand traps of the mind. For example:

Stress, excess and change

Let's try to get *more* stress, excess and change into our lives. There are so many books telling us not to do this, not to do that, cut down, slow down, quit, stop, control, stabilize, that people are turned off. The plethora of literature has become ridiculous and almost comical instead of helpful.

We're struggling and wrestling so much, to try to get rid of stress, that we're creating more in the process. We're attempting to be moderate rather than excessive in everything we do, to the point of becoming wishy-washy. We're accepting without question the point of view put forward by sociologists that everyone resists change.

Let's examine these admonitions from a totally different perspective.

Stress

Obviously, there is an enormous difference between stress that causes distress and stress that does not. Most of us attempt to rid ourselves of stress when our real problem is the way we are handling stress. It's not the stress that wipes us out—it's the *distress*. Dr. Hans Selye, author of *Stress Without Distress* and one of the world's leading authorities on stress and its effects on the human body, proposed a different approach. He said, "You can't rid yourself of stress, no matter how hard you try. It takes conflict to make the heart beat. The trick is to avoid using up too much of your general adaption syndrome (GAS)."

We can run out of GAS. But without any stress, our hearts won't be beating for long. Stressful activity, like exercise and anger, makes the heart pound. Conflict causes the blood to run through veins. Systolic action is inherently stressful but periodically necessary to live.

So, with GAS in mind, we will often say: Pile on the stress. Get as much stress in your life as possible. Test your triple bypass to see if it's working. Experts agree that people bring dangerous levels of distress upon themselves by excessive worrying about the stress that wasn't going to hurt them in the first place. A vicious cycle.

Therefore, accept stress. Embrace and appreciate it. Don't resist or deny it. We're going to have it whether we want it or not. Politicians won't go away, hotels will still lose your reservations and flights will be overbooked. (We had a friend who was so angry being bumped from a flight with his family to Hawaii that he started his own executive airline.)

One of the most pleasurable human activities produces intense stress. It makes our hearts nearly pound out of our chest, our skin flush, our pupils dilate and our breathing become rapid. None of us would be here without this type of stress. If our point of view is causing you stress, enjoy it—but don't get distressed.

Do something. Go for it. Lay it on. Stress yourself out of the box!

Excess

There has rarely ever been any great achievement without excess. Do things to excess. We're not referring to overeating, drinking too much or consuming harmful drugs. What we mean is resisting the temptation to be philosophically moderate. Moderation dilutes a virtue and enhances a vice. Examples:

- Moderate truth.
- Moderate honesty.
- Moderate integrity.
- Moderate crime.
- Moderate child abuse.
- Moderate intolerance.

If it is a virtue, we want as much of it as we can get. If it's a vice, we want to get rid of it all, not just part of it. When we talk about excess, we're referring to concepts, values and standards. One of the worst concepts in the world from this viewpoint is moderation. Whatever we decide is worth doing is worth doing to excess. Pile on the stress. Make the heart pound. Indulge in constructive concepts, values and ideas with excessive commitment. Get worked up over something.

Change

There is nothing more misunderstood than how people react to change. We are told that people don't like change and resist it. Actually, people love change if it brings hope of something better. Without change, we have sameness and boredom. We all anticipate new experiences that bring variety and enrichment to our lives.

The trap of positive thinking

The philosophy of positive thinking may have damaged more people than any disease known to medical science. It's a sand trap that boxes in millions of creative hopefuls by causing faulty thinking.

Positive thinking too often becomes a substitute for *realistic* thinking. How? By claiming we don't have a problem when we do, or claiming we have something when we don't. Positive thinking, then, becomes wishful thinking, setting us up to sabotage our own best interests.

> *"If we believe strongly enough, if we never have*
> *any doubt, we can do anything if we visualize it."*
>
> *"If we really accept, if we're really positive, if we*
> *have complete faith—we can overcome anything."*

These injunctions are only partially true. The part that's untrue can harm us. We believe the human spirit is indomitable and can accomplish virtually anything, but logicians will add that we can do nothing outside the realm of truth and reality.

A positive attitude should result from realistic thinking—overcoming obstacles, matching our dreams with a doable action plan and even promoting healing. We've seen too many people's spirits broken by positive thinking carried to extremes. Many people have thought positive thoughts, tried and prayed, only to suffer the fate they hoped fervently to avoid. Ignoring a strange lump—certain that positive thoughts will make it go away—is a foolish and dangerous thing to do.

We're in no way criticizing the inspirational messages of Dr. Norman Vincent Peale, author of the 1952 classic *The Power of Positive Thinking*. We knew Dr. Peale and his wife, Ruth, through some of life's most memorable moments and intimate experiences. Our long-time friends John and Brian Palmer, who represented Dr. Peale for many years, arranged opportunities for us to see them on various occasions.

John Palmer remembers when Dr. Peale and Mike were speaking at the same convention and had back-to-back hotel rooms. Mike woke up one morning to the sound of someone singing "Oh, What a Beautiful Morning" at the top of his lungs. Of course it was Norman Peale. Mike nearly cut himself shaving while laughing at Dr. Peale's exuberance for life.

During their occasional conversations, Dr. Peale acknowledged to Mike that the original concept of positive thinking had been distorted to ridiculous extremes by some people. He felt strongly that positive thinking should never involve a denial of reality. Reverend Peale, while insisting that complete faith and God's help could produce miracles, told Mike, "Positive thinking should never become a substitute for action."

The debate will continue over positive thinking. We can't possibly resolve it here. We merely hope to raise awareness about a clearer understanding of the subject. Additional truths about deeply ingrained beliefs help us to think out of the box. We can also seek a positive attitude by practicing valid thinking. We can even add faith to the equation for those who are spiritual. Dr. Roy A. Burkhart said, "Faith is reason grown courageous."

Too serious, too stuffy

Dating game contestants are asked to name the qualities they look for in an ideal mate. They all say, "A sense of humor is a must." Most of us don't like people who are too stuffy or too serious. They put a damper on everything. Creativity goes out the window with these wet blankets.

Humor is often a scarce commodity in the business world, because we get too occupied with the bottom line. Humor is the unmasking of hypocrisy. Laughter doesn't necessarily mean that people are goofing off, but rather enjoying what they are doing. Humor reveals conditions that are screwed up, which forces us to look at problems the way they actually are rather than bluffing or covering up. Humor helps us to think out of the box.

A story featured in *USA Today* reported that the average child laughs about 400 times per day. The article went on to say the average adult laughs only 15 times per day. What happened to the other 385 laughs?

Dr. Norman Cousins has written numerous books about the healing nature of laughter. Laughter actually helped save his life when he was seriously ill and written off as incurable by his physician. He rented Charlie Chaplin movies and roared at them. A seriously ill man on death's doorstep laughed, instead of moping around, complaining and bemoaning his fate. Cousins called this laughter therapy. To paraphrase Cousins' refreshing concept, the unseen tears of laughter bathe our insides with healing chemicals. Research has verified the healing power and positive health benefits of laughter.

The importance of laughter and humor in the workplace can't be emphasized enough. After countless experiences with corporate brainstorming sessions, we need no further proof that the most powerful, out-of-the-box thinking occurs when people are loosened up by laughter.

If you read *The Bridges of Madison County* or see the movie and don't cry, you're probably dead already. We cry when something triggers our emotions regarding what we care about deeply. Laughter is similar to this. Have you ever laughed so hard you cried? You weren't crying because you were sad necessarily. Your emotions were running so deep, your body was confused. Most people laugh more easily than they cry. Children's emotions are more evenly balanced between laughing and crying, often switching between the two like a swinging gate. When you laugh too hard, your body might release so many chemicals it thinks it's reached the mythical crying place.

Emotions can become overwhelming at times to the point we don't know if we're happy or sad or both. That was the case when Mike's troop ship from Korea docked in San Francisco. The young women singing on the pier, the people there to greet the soldiers finally coming home, their own emotions swirling inside of them. Clinical counselors describe a time of tremendous emotional outpouring and emotional confusion as an *affect storm,* which simply means a storm of feelings. We can think of many times our ships have been tossed to and fro in an affect storm. Yet, laughter is a positive alternative that's constantly available to us. We need to make an effort to use it more.

Some people mistakenly believe seriousness portrays intelligence and legitimacy. They believe being serious is a requirement for being taken seriously. But the evidence indicates that a smile wins more often than a frown—if it's sincere. Obvious, but true. We often tell our audiences there are more points in our humor than there are in our points. So if you miss the points in our humor, you'll miss the points of our points. Most people get the point.

Jim Newton, author of *Uncommon Friends,* told us Henry Ford used to write down his jokes and take them over to Thomas Edison's house and read them to him. Jim said Edison really loved a good laugh. He even reminded himself in his journals, "Tell a good joke to the men in the laboratory." A rich sense of humor is reported to be a common thread among many outstanding inventors. Laughter and humor are definitely common among out-of-the-box thinkers.

We regularly recommend to our business clients that they tell a joke—a good joke, that is—or a funny story at their daily briefings. Diane often has a "joke of the day" at her daily staff briefings. Situational humor, where we laugh at ourselves, is usually the best because we enjoy watching others poke fun at themselves. Mark Twain said, "The reason people laugh at weddings and cry at funerals is because they're not the ones involved."

In the project and design work we do, we have both observed that breakthrough ideas consistently come sooner when a team is having fun together and not taking themselves or their task too seriously. Uptight people make for uptight solutions that lack oil and juice. In other words, they're dried up. Ask your teammates, "Am I a 'wet' or am I a 'dry'?" They'll tell you. (Lawyers fall in the middle; they're usually moist.)

In a planning charrette[1] we conducted for a Johnson & Johnson Company with Tom Guest and Ken Dobler, we learned the common thread among our client's award-winning sales reps was a well-developed sense of humor. People loved to be around them and, obviously, people loved to buy from them.

In the Disney motion picture *Mary Poppins,* there is a wonderful scene devoted entirely to laughter. The scene features the chimney

---

[1]An intensive work out on a project using creative thinking techniques.

sweep Bert having a tea party on the ceiling and singing the Sherman brothers' hit song, "I Love to Laugh." Another little known fact about highly creative people: They love to laugh their way out of the box!

Keep an informed mind

The maxim "keep an open mind" sounds so correct. But open minds are often empty minds. Open minds can contain ambiguous convictions, vague concepts and unresolved issues. Also, open minds can be filled with trash. The *informed* mind is also open to new ideas, but recognizes and filters out detrimental thoughts.

The informed mind will share thoughts and ideas with others, but usually exercise caution with harmful thoughts. The informed mind is decided, not undecided, about issues, but will consider them further through research and argumentation. We hear many people say, "I am an open-minded person." However, the unspoken subtext is often, "As long as you agree with me." Thinking out of the box requires having an informed mind before we can truly be open-minded.

Be afraid of failure, but not to fail

If it's been said once, it's been said 10,000 times in books and lectures, "Don't be afraid to fail." Yet, to be afraid of failure is not necessarily the same as being afraid to fail. This will sound like double-talk until you analyze the proposition more deeply. You may be afraid *to* fail, but you're afraid *of* failure because failure can cause irreparable damage to the lives touched by its consequences. It's the fear *of* failure that often motivates us to try harder, use greater care and evaluate our judgments. Thoughtfulness is a key part of solid thinking.

Conversely, the fear of failure does not need to create in us the fear *to* fail. Originality is achieved by continuous experimenting in which failure is part of the process. We must be ever-mindful that mixing the wrong ingredients can create a critical mess leading to a meltdown. Be afraid of failure, but don't be afraid to fail.

Missions without methods

A mission statement, to be effective, must contain the method to make it happen. Also, a mission statement containing buzzwords, clichés and bromides will undoubtedly fail. For example:

"We are a seamless company with empowered teams in a boundaryless culture of shared values that is continually reengineering our core business with our core competency."

Unfortunately, this is an actual mission statement of a large company. This was created by a committee, mistakenly called a team, who was assigned the task of curing everything wrong with the company in six months through a new mission statement. You know that nothing got better at this company as a result of this exercise.

We work closely with companies to create Team Centers™[2] and devise and implement creative programs to help transform or improve their cultures. We've observed that people are extremely sensitive to being put on like this and to the broken promises that result. We see firsthand people who are shown fancy mission statements and then sent to exhaustive training, only to return to an organization that doesn't respect or really want fresh ideas. Consequently, every time people are promised change, and then let down, they become more cynical and harder to inspire and motivate.

Clearly, the finest concepts in the world won't get off the ground if the foundation isn't established first. It is incumbent upon us to create an authentic climate before even the best organizational ideas will catch on enough to become part of the culture. New processes alone won't help. Neither will new techniques. Speed, as well, will not replace a sense of direction or vision or mission.

Sincerity of purpose is the foundation upon which any successful mission statement should be based.

---

[2]Team Center™ is a trademark of Intellectual Equities, Inc. It is a creative environment that provides resources for individuals and teams to promote creativity, teamwork and innovation.

"Experience the things that I've experienced
and you'll do what I did—build a hospital."
—Dr. Albert Schweitzer

Life's experiences spawn our passions—strong feelings of love, hate, hostility and sympathy. True life experiences form the foundation of personal dreams, goals, objectives, missions and visions. The nature and intensity of these experiences, constructive or destructive, determine the zest and zeal with which we pursue our mission. Neither you nor anyone in your organization needs prodding from superficial motivational hype or shallow bromides from self-proclaimed gurus to get going. Getting involved raises our temperature. Being informed allows us to size up the challenge. And creating something new inspires our soul. It's about doing. It's about action.

The mission with the method

When he was 10 years old, Mike's son John asked him, "Dad, could you teach me how to be more creative?"

"Why do you want to be more creative?" Mike asked.

"So I can be a better soccer player," John shot back. "My coach says I need to be creative to be a really good soccer player." Mike saw an ideal opportunity to introduce John to the nine-dot exercise he used for demonstrating creative thinking to others.

The nine-dot box exercise was chosen as the logo for the Creative Thinking Association of America because the solution represents the creative thought process so well, and most people are familiar with the illustration. Why more people don't apply the solution to their personal and professional problems is mystifying. Nonetheless, it's always helpful to remind ourselves of how easy it is to fall victim to old habits and limited thinking. It's very common to find ourselves sealed in the box, even though we know how to think ourselves out. Life naturally seals us in with invisible but very real barriers.

The instructions for the exercise are:

1. Connect all nine dots using no more than four straight lines.
2. The dots cannot be repositioned.
3. The connecting line must be drawn in one continuous stroke.
4. Leave the pencil on the paper until all lines have been drawn.

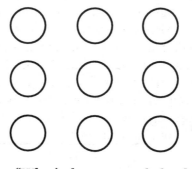

John asked Mike, "What's the concept behind the answer?" Mike explained that the concept behind the solutions is to not allow our thinking to be contained and limited by imaginary boundaries. Thinking outside of boundaries and limitations is what creative thinking is clearly about. "Can I see an example of how to do it?" he persisted.

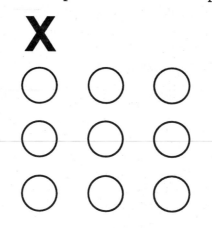

Mike then showed John an example of the concept, which is called a model. Creative thinking analyzes concepts, demonstrates with examples and produces models. The nine-part formula for success is a model for you to use.

John looked carefully and thoughtfully at the example. He was apparently intrigued and inspired—two natural results of creative thinking. "Dad, don't do it for me. Let me figure it out from here, okay? I can do it."

His remark reminded Mike of how quickly creativity is stifled when we intervene by doing other people's thinking for them. People can't learn how to think out of the box unless they're doing their own thinking.

Several days passed before John approached his dad with the solution:

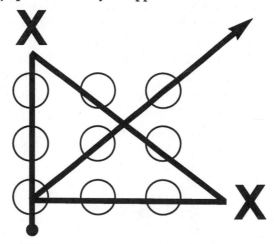

He had added the second point outside the box to complete the exercise. Mike felt satisfied that John had figured out the concept and made it meaningful for himself. His creative appetite was now stimulated, more than could be realized.

John became a skilled soccer player by going where the ball was going instead of where it *was*, just like Wayne Gretsky goes to where the hockey puck is *going* to be. That's thinking out of the box. Are you focused on where the market's going to be rather than where it is? Think about it.

Three years later, John, then 13, came to Mike with another burning question. "Do you have a name for the point at the X, the first place you drew the line to?" he asked and pointed to it on the model.

The first point you draw your line to is *vision* or *mission*. You can't think out of any box without a vision or a mission. John immediately caught Mike's drift and added, "And connecting all the dots by thinking out of the box is the method of how to do it now!" He got it.

In fact, Mike says John taught *him* the idea that the method must be included. By the time you've connected mission and method, you're halfway to your solution. John completed the exercise and the concept on his own. He understood that a mission with a method stimulates thinking out of the box. (Missions without methods rarely get implemented. Therefore, you should not develop a mission statement without developing a *method* statement.) You can imagine how exciting it was to see his growth and understanding! You will find it just as exciting every time you help someone to go beyond their imaginary boundaries and think out of the box.

Danny Cox, author and professional speaker, and his wife, Theo, are two of our best friends. They are both remarkable individuals who focus on building relationships with people from every walk of life. We have spent countless hours with Danny and Theo, sharing stories, ideas and friends. They brought Dr. Robert Schuller to our Creative Living Center for a memorable evening of dining and philosophical discussion. Danny also introduced us to their best friends Jim and Ellie Newton. In sharing their friendships with us, Danny and Theo gave us two new friends who have made a tremendous impact on our lives. Jim and Ellie helped us begin to appreciate what a lost art friendship is fast becoming. Jim was a good friend of Thomas Edison, Henry Ford, Harvey Firestone, Dr. Alexis Carrel and Charles Lindbergh, and his book *Uncommon Friends* is a revealing account of his life with these great people.

After Danny sent us Jim's book, he arranged for a meeting with Jim and Ellie in Fort Myers, Florida. The entire experience was nothing short of a red-letter day for us—a breathtaking, inspirational moment in every way.

The art of friendship

The computer craze has ushered in another term for friendships and relationships—called networking. The term was popularized by John Naisbitt in his book *Megatrends*.

We like networking. But we also like the time-honored art of personal friendship, where friends visit your house and take trips with you. One of the best-kept secrets of highly successful people is that they thrive on friendships. The art of friendship has some basic tenets:

- Be a friend to yourself, which readies you to be a friend to others.
- Reach out to others by being open and forthcoming. Hold no grudges.
- Try not to compete with friends, but rejoice in their pleasures. Avoid artificial positioning and control.
- Be prepared to grow and change your life because of your friendships.

Jim Newton invited us to a conference in Caux, Switzerland. We were inspired by the people we met there. We stayed at Mountain House, which is high above the resort town of Montreux. This pristine setting is reachable only by cog railroad, and has a spectacular view of the French Alps.

We ate breakfast one morning with Vladimir Suprun, a Russian philosophy professor, and with Tianethone Chantharasy, a former Cambodian ambassador. Tianethone made the statement that the U.S. is really the only superpower left. Then he added, "But you need to add the word 'great.' The U.S. is a great superpower. Do you know why the U.S. is a great superpower?" he asked us. He gave two reasons. "First, you are the most generous nation on earth; you help everybody. Second, you forgive your enemies. You even help your enemies rebuild." Another well-kept secret of people who think out of the box—they are generous and forgiving.

Here are additional sand traps that may keep you imprisoned in a box:

stalling	ethnocentrism	imposing values
ignorance	ambivalence	jumping on buzzwords
false friendship	using jargon	arrogance
elitism	indifference	misrepresentation
lip service	lying	no closure
manipulation	knowing it all	no deliverables
condescension	being antisocial	speaking in platitudes
deceit	bullying	hiding things

Vision

Vision is a crucial component in the formula for success. It holds the keys to the future. The inspirational lives we look to for guidance remind us of this time and time again. The following incident will illustrate our point.

At Disney studios in Burbank, California, Mike could gaze out of his office window, across Buena Vista Street, to St. Joseph's Hospital where Walt Disney died. The morning he died, Mike was talking on the telephone when he saw the flag being lowered over at the hospital around 8:20 a.m. His death was preceded by an amazing incident that reportedly took place the night before in Walt's hospital room.

A journalist, knowing Walt was seriously ill, persisted in getting an interview with Walt and was frustrated on numerous occasions by the hospital staff. When he finally managed to get into the room, Walt couldn't sit up in bed or talk above a whisper. Walt instructed the reporter to lie down on the bed, next to him, so he could whisper in the reporter's ear. For the next 30 minutes, Walt and the journalist lay side by side as Walt referred to an imaginary map of Walt Disney World on the ceiling above the bed.

Walt pointed out where he planned to place various attractions and buildings. He talked about transportation, hotels, restaurants and many other parts of his vision for a property that wouldn't open to the public for another six years.

We told this reporter's moving experience, relayed through a nurse, to each one of our organizational development (OD) groups...the story of how a man who lay dying in the hospital whispered in the reporter's ear for 30 minutes describing his vision for the future and the role he would play in it for generations to come.

This is the way to live—believing so much in your vision that even when you're dying, you whisper it into another person's ear.

Norman Brinker: Informed

Norman Brinker is a brilliant restaurateur and consummate innovator of new dining features. He formerly headed the restaurant division at Pillsbury before founding Brinker International. Of all the people we've worked with over the years, he truly exemplifies the principle of staying informed and keeping others informed through participation. We've talked with many restaurant people about Norman and always find him highly regarded by those who know him and his exceptional work. "The more people are like themselves, the less they're like anyone else, which makes them unique." Our observation about originality is a fitting description of Norman Brinker—a unique person.

We can hear Norman now, in his deep Texas accent, saying, "You're not talking about me, are you? I'm just a real basic type of person." He is down-to-earth and sincere. Like Roy Disney, Norman's low-key style fools many people into misjudging his razor-sharp mind, deep philosophical nature and genius business acumen. His personal philosophy is simple yet profound:

"Most of us have been knocked down a lot, but when we're down we get up and finish what we started."

Norman Brinker invented the concept of casual dining and made countless innovations in the restaurant industry. He and his team have built Brinker International into a magnificent company in just a short time with Chili's, Romano's Macaroni Grill and other successful formats. He gave us Steak and Ale restaurants, which pioneered the development of the salad bar. The incredible fajita was popularized at Chili's.

Norman and his wife, Nancy, received two awards from the Creative Thinking Association of America at its awards event in Houston, Texas. The Association acknowledges outstanding creative contributions each year. We chatted with Nancy at dinner about our experiences with Norman.

We met Norman for the first time at the Burger King managers' meeting in Lake Tahoe when he was Burger King's leader. Gary Link and Mike Jenkins, two of his associates, hired us to conduct a seminar on applying creativity to the restaurant industry. In fact, it was at that meeting Mike made a challenging comment that launched the burger wars of the 1980s. Mike was joking around with the Burger King managers and said, "You guys at Burger King ought to bend McDonald's arches; bend them 'till they crack." Norman seized on the idea and said, "Let's do it." And with that, he launched one of the most proactive and aggressive marketing campaigns the fast-food industry has ever experienced. That was our first exposure to Norman's infectious can-do attitude which inspires anyone who meets him.

Norman's leadership gave Burger King's sales a significant spike, reaffirming the power of strong leadership based on inspired management. Pleased with his organization's success and motivated to grow further, he hired Vance Design to work with the Link-Jenkins team to create fresh ideas for a Mexican restaurant. That's when we flew off to Dallas to begin an unforgettable adventure with Norman's people. When we conduct or participate in a successful project, we always make wonderful new friends. Our experience in Dallas was no exception.

A restaurant is born

We immediately set up a Team Center in a hotel ballroom along the LBJ Freeway in Dallas. The space we used was about 150 feet long and 40 feet wide. We equipped the room with Displayed Thinking®1 boards as well as supplies and resources to design the new restaurant format. People began to feel involved as soon as the Team Center was established. It quickly became a dynamic hub of activity.

We set up a workroom in the adjacent ballroom to display concept models of the new format, costume design, table setups and even an area to bring

---

[1]Displayed Thinking® is a registered trademark of Intellectual Equities, Inc. It is a method of visualizing concepts, ideas and facts used in planning, creating and working.

in the food we considered for the menu. The environment was supercharged and the stream of ideas was outstanding, both in quantity and quality.

It was in the midst of this "happening" that the real essence of Norman Brinker emerged before our very eyes. The creative team process has that effect on people. The Team Center was filled with idea boards, including the master plan, promotions and financials. Next door, the models were on display and lighted with temporary theatrical lighting. The dining table was set up for a test lunch sampling proposed menu features.

When you see a fire...

We completed an overview briefing on the project for Norman, who continually added ideas, then adjourned for lunch in the model room next door. We were joined at the candle-lit table by several other executives. We were served virgin margaritas and chips in paper-lined baskets. Everything was going smoothly until the paper in a chips basket caught fire from the candle on the table.

No one at the table moved or said a word; they just observed. The fire grew until it was about to consume the entire basket, but still no one in the group moved. Finally, Norman broke the frozen tableau by putting out the flames with his water glass and cloth napkin. One team member said, "You can tell who the entrepreneur is in this bunch—the one who did something about the fire." Norman said, "When you see a fire, put it out." This was a demonstration of entrepreneurial thinking expressed most eloquently.

Informed and involved

Following this successful experience, Norman asked us to help him on a Burger King project again. He acknowledged that the restaurant chain had been knocked down some, but that "when you're down, you need to get up and finish what you started." We scheduled a seminar at Burger King headquarters in Miami. Norman held a breakfast meeting at his club in Palm Beach to map out the plan of action. It was a five-star breakfast in a perfect setting with good food, exceptional company and a mission to challenge us.

Norman was full of philosophy that morning because the Burger King assignment was a monumental challenge in a highly competitive industry. Like other effective leaders, when faced with a significant challenge, Norman Brinker fell back on his basic beliefs. He said, "People have to be sincere in business. We can't go very far if we're not sincere, because how far we go depends on the feelings our team has about us. Success with customers is the direct result of success with our employees."

His point was to keep employees informed and involved in the process to improve the product. He felt the managers would respect Mike's Disney background and pay attention to what was a foreign concept to them. Norman appreciated the difference between experience and theory. He predicted the managers would have more respect for experience than just theory. He went on to explain that getting back up on your feet after being knocked down requires having a recognizable and achievable goal in front of you. He pointed out that too many people focus on the problem and not the goal.

"Go around the problem to the goal," he said. "Go for the touchdown. Do an end run on the problem. Finish. Too many people don't finish the game." Norman has made many notable observations, including: "You have to be worthy of leadership. You can't bluff your way through it." He was explaining that you have to have leadership qualities in order to lead and assist the team toward reaching its goal.

Norman Brinker was almost killed when his horse fell on him during a polo match. He lapsed into a coma and it was touch-and-go for many agonizing days. Nancy, his wife, and a competent medical team nursed him back to health and he eventually returned to action. He knew firsthand about being knocked down and getting back up.

We have found that the simplest injunctions are often the best practices. Norman Brinker's best practices include:

- Emphasis on training and education.
- Entrepreneurship.
- Creativity.
- Being people-centered.
- Good sportsmanship.
- Experimenting.
- Acting—not just talking.
- Sincerity.
- Finishing the game.
- Great leadership qualities.

CHAPTER 2

Tools for opening the box

What we do is determined by what we are.

What we are is determined by what we think.

What we think is determined by what we experience.

What we experience is determined by what we are exposed to and what we do with that exposure.

There are three valuable creative tools that can be used to open the box. These tools will help you apply the creative formula for success you're about to discover for stimulating creativity. To best utilize the tools, it's important to know their origins, how and why they were developed, where we got the ideas for them and how you can effectively use them to think creatively. The three most valuable tools are:

1. Category note-taking.
2. Thinking in all five senses.
3. Working in color.

Using the tools

When we want to improve anything and really make it better, one of the most effective ways is to start by examining what's right about it. As ingenious as the Disneyland attractions were, Walt Disney continually worked to perfect them. He began the task of improvement by considering what was right about them and what made them truly outstanding.

As he examined the strengths of his attractions, he would discover that important features that were missing gradually began to become clear to him. The same dynamic principle holds true when working on any project. Unfortunately, most people, when faced with a similar challenge, begin by critiquing and analyzing, focusing instead on the negative and, much of the time, miss discovering the singular features that makes a work truly meritorious.

Walt's unusual approach was a unique method for thinking out of the box. The Blue Bayou restaurant and the Pirates of the Caribbean adventure, as you experience them today, include not only original design elements but also the special additions. Despite the overwhelming scope of the attraction, the subtle, almost insignificant fireflies bring a touch of realism and enchantment to the experience. Walt's unique methods and insight made it possible to find what was missing.

One memorable evening, Walt was conducting a briefing on the entrance complex to Walt Disney World. We had been working on design ideas with a management development group for many, many weeks. Walt dropped into our team unit a couple of times during that process to check on our progress. He talked and informally worked with us on various aspects, rather than merely sending us away to come back with the answers. Walt had a modified collaborative style of leadership, even though he knew exactly what feel he wanted. He kept sparks of creativity and enthusiasm flashing because he really got in and "mixed it up" with the team. His enthusiasm and personal participation inspired the involvement of others and remains an exemplary model for any enlightened leader.

Category note-taking

In the meeting that specifically comes to mind, Walt sat down with us and placed several piles of index cards around the team table casually. He then spread out a number of colored pencils and began discussing the entrance complex and what we had come up with by asking the question, "What's good about the concepts you've developed on the entrance complex so far?"

Everyone on the team began writing down what we thought were the significant design features of the entrance complex on the index cards. We then began to assemble the cards under the categories that had been established.

As soon as we began considering what was right about our design for the entrance complex for Walt Disney World, the missing elements began to emerge. We had something concrete to work with right away. The concept of working in categories was born out of this experience. Form followed function and tools began to take shape for opening the box.

Thinking in strictly linear patterns (sometimes jokingly referred to as winged-tip thinking) is traditionally considered to be the domain of engineers, accountants and attorneys. More natural thinking patterns tend to jump around from subject to subject, looking at the same object or idea from various angles, analyzing a variety of possibilities and considering this or that alternative—even drifting into other subjects along the way.

Despite how the mind may naturally function, conventional education trains us to take notes straight down the page, following a left margin on ruled paper. Add a yellow legal tablet and you're taking notes like a lawyer...A before B, B before C, 1 before 2 and 2 before 3. Category note-taking, as fully developed at the Creative Thinking Association, is an added improvement to note-taking, which links it to the concept of Displayed Thinking.

We are not suggesting to arbitrarily abandon linear note-taking altogether. We urge you to add category note-taking to your box of creative tools. In the creative thinking process, the category method fosters high retention, sensible arrangement of materials, easier recall and a clearer picture of the material being studied. The category method enhances the development of images by giving otherwise linear concepts shape and dimension.

The Displayed Thinking format in the figure on page 40 is used for category note-taking.[2] Outstanding teachers often use this format to outline the main categories they plan to cover in a lecture or discussion. Various categories and ideas for the topic to be developed are placed in the subject box. The subjects are like general categories. The following headings are suggested subject categories for the Displayed Thinking form:

1. Major Points. Throughout this book, you'll find many major points used as subheadings. On the Displayed Thinking form, you may want to list the major points to make it easier to identify and review.

2. Resources. Resources can take on many forms—books, movies, products, conversations with knowledgeable people—all sorts of items and information that relate and contribute to the major categories you've identified.

3. Recommendations. As soon as major categories begin to emerge, the question arises, "What do I do with this material?" Throughout this book, you'll want to note how concepts are utilized. You'll want to begin taking field trips and dreaming up new and unique ways of applying creative ideas to your personal life.

4. Definitions. What do certain words mean within the context of special uses and interpretations? It's important to write down new definitions as they arise for future reference and understanding.

5. Applications. Ideas and concepts that emerge under one scenario might have valuable applications in other areas you haven't thought of. Applicability of creative concepts can be a creative process of its own. Category note-taking gives you a method to single them out for tracking purposes.

6. Background. It's a good idea to take notes regarding the background and origin of the ideas and concepts you're dealing with. This is

---

[2]These convenient sheets are available in various sizes and colors through the Creative Thinking Association, 16600 Sprague Road, Suite 120, Cleveland, OH 44130; (216) 243-5576.

best accomplished through stories, examples, profiles, principles and illustrations.

7. Miscellaneous. There are always ideas and materials that don't fit neatly under the other categories. That doesn't mean they're unimportant. They should be noted for possible future inclusion.

You might want to add additional categories for note-taking that reflect your own interests. A list of particulars or specific ideas relating to the subject are entered in the details boxes. The details support and examine the subject. When you're finished, your notes will be organized in their proper categories.

Category note-taking is designed to stimulate creativity and promote flexibility. It's the alternative to the limitations of linear thinking. Your specific needs should be reflected in how you structure and use the Displayed Thinking format. A fundamental part of your best practices for creativity should include category note-taking as a technique.

Sensanation: thinking in all five senses

The many categories considered by the organizational development group for the Walt Disney World entrance complex is what made the entrance complex begin to look inviting. Soon we realized that people don't focus on a single physical sensation at any given time. Although only one sensation might be working on the conscious level, the other four senses are constantly at work on the subconscious level. We found ourselves working with sight—what the entrance complex would look like. Before long, we were considering not only the physical appearance of the entrance complex, but how it would feel to the visitor.

We recognized right away that the entrance complex had to be thought of as more than just a place to enter, but just as importantly as an experience for the five senses. We attempted to stimulate our imaginations—to see images of the creative thoughts as we considered them. Mental pictures take form as visions and solutions to problems and needs. Yet, there is far more than only imagination to consider in creating original thoughts.

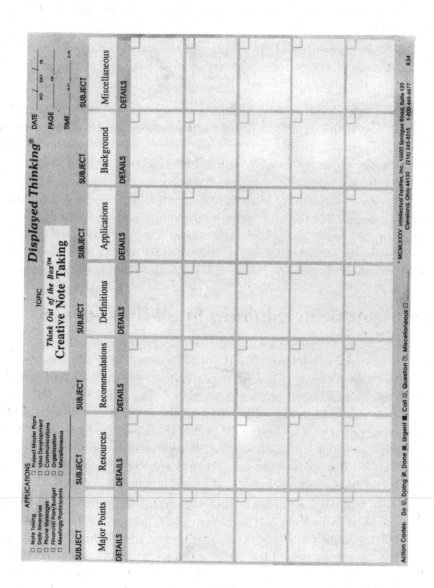

As our team contemplated what sounds Walt Disney World visitors would hear as they entered the park and if the entrance complex would be appealing to the other senses of touch, taste and smell as well as sight and sound, we began searching for a word more expansive than imagination. Image-ination means the forming of images in context of creative thought. To us, imagination came to mean the forming of an image. To incorporate all five senses, we coined the term "sensanation," which means simultaneously thinking in the additional senses of sight, sound, taste, touch and smell.[3]

Sensanation gives us a wider range to scan our thought waves. Sensanation must be cued or triggered by some mental device to engage the creative process. Such cuing or triggering devices offer glimpses of the creative formula, causing a chain reaction in the mental process. Cues and triggers are found within a single sense or a combination of senses. You can become more proficient with the use of sensanation by regularly employing the concept. Think of a subject from the perspective of sight, sound, touch, taste and smell. Consider each sense separately at first, then in different combinations with one another.

If you were designing a restaurant with a New Orleans theme, like the Blue Bayou restaurant in Disneyland, what would you picture in your mind? The Louisiana bayou country? Shadowy swamps? And what else? No shadowy, mysterious swamp is complete without fireflies darting about, their tails blinking a pulsating and erratic rhythm.

But the fireflies were only one added feature of the Blue Bayou environment at Disneyland. What about the distinctive aromas lingering in the air of Old New Orleans? Roasting coffee with chicory adulterating the brew adds to the unmistakable ambiance of the French Quarter. The chicory aroma of fresh coffee was circulated through the restaurant's air-conditioning system to trigger the sensation of smell. Anyone who has had the pleasure of dining in the Blue Bayou restaurant at Disneyland can probably recall the strains of that Dixieland jazz music in the background, combined with the distinctive sounds of crickets chirping and a lone banjo, plucking out a lazy melody in the distance.

---

[3]A good resource book for better understanding the five senses is *Natural History of the Senses* by Diane Ackerman (New York: Random House).

Overhead are ever-changing cloud patterns. Where other ambitious restaurateurs might paint clouds on the ceiling, Walt Disney's indoor sky above diners' heads features moving clouds. The lights in the windows of the bayou shacks flicker, adding authenticity to the ambiance.

These design features, and numerous others, including the iron dining furniture, add up to a complete sensanation experience. Each sensory element—sight, sound, smell, touch and taste—is subtle, just as it is in nature. No single effect overwhelms the others. Even as you experience the environment, you might not identify the various triggers to your sensanation responses, but you will definitely have an experience of being there, as if you've been transported to a unique place and time. That's one reason why it's usually the children, with their imaginations closer to the surface, who notice the fireflies first.

Creativity is the making of the new and
the rearranging of the old in a new way.

Body speak: blushing

The right word, sound, smell, visual image, taste or touch can trigger an emotional reaction that envelops your entire body. Instant sensanational reactions can cause blood to rush to the epidermal layer of your skin, producing a blush. In a millisecond, given the necessary sensory stimulation, your entire body can turn red. Blushing is unmistakable evidence that something sensanational is occurring in your life at that moment. It could be rage, embarrassment or any number of things. The blush is simply your body's way of involuntarily crying out in that moment—something sent an unconscious cue to trigger the reaction. We can't make ourselves blush and we can't stop a blush in progress.

Body speak: goose bumps

Other triggers, such as someone dragging their fingernails across a backboard, the performance of a stirring piece of music, a patriotic moment of pride, a phenomenal moment at the ballet or perhaps a riveting speech can produce goose bumps—another instant, involuntary body response to a stimulus.

Body speak: chills

Being frightened by a scary moment in a Stephen King movie, suddenly coming across a tragic auto accident, hearing a startling sound in the middle of the night or experiencing some other unexpected and shocking experience usually results in a sudden drop in temperature, otherwise known as a chill. The chill is symptomatic of shock and is the reverse of the blush. Whereas a blush causes blood to rush to the epidermal layer of skin, a chill results from blood temporarily evacuating the outer extremities.

Blushing, goose bumps and chills each indicate the body is reacting involuntarily to a sensanational stimulus. It's surprising more people don't use sensanation as a conscious tool, since so many people experience these common human responses. It's one of the most effective ways to stimulate creativity, which gives us a strategic advantage. So many human conditions are ready and waiting to assist us if we simply take into account the ways the human mind and body respond.

From the mouths of babes

Mike will never forget a beautiful moment when his daughter, Vanessa, was 7 years old. We were having dinner with a group that included Steve Jobs, cofounder of Apple Computer, at the Pine Lake Trout Club in Ohio. At one point, Steve turned to Vanessa and asked how she liked her Apple Computer.

Mike was sure he was expecting a standard answer from a typical little girl. Instead, Steve got a spontaneous answer from Vanessa, who was really in tune with her senses.

She said, "Steve, it doesn't smell very good."

Taken slightly off guard, he asked what she meant.

"It smells like burnt plastic. I take scratch 'n' sniff pages out of my scratch 'n' sniff book and tape them to the keyboard when I'm working on it so it will smell better."

Then she looked straight at Steve and chided, "You're smart—can't you build a computer that smells good?"

She got his attention. We can't think of a better example to illustrate how important it is to consider the total sensanation experience when designing products, working environments, retail environments, recreational environments, living environments—you name it.

The five senses: sight

It's said that a picture is worth a thousand words. We believe an experience is worth a thousand pictures. Seeing can mean a variety of things to different people. The list can include associations like these:

afterimage	appearance	apperception
beautiful	blind	cast an eye
catch an eye	display	distance
distinguish	draw a bead	exhibition
eye	eyeball	eyeful
eyeshot	eyesight	feast your eyes
field of vision	first sight	gander
gawk	gaze	get a look at
glance	goggle	lay eyes on
on the face of it	once over	out of sight
outlook	peep	perception
range of vision	scenes	see eye-to-eye
seeing	spectacle	spot
survey	ugly	viewing
visibility	vision	witness

There are, of course, many more sight-related terms we could add to this list, but these few give an idea of how a simple thought can spawn related ideas and issues. We know that the technique of visualizing means to mentally picture something we wish to create. The five-sensing or sensanation technique is an exercise in visualization that incorporates each of the five senses in the mental simulation. Put another way: Sensanation is the creation of a virtual experience.

The late Ohio State football coach, Woody Hayes, was known for his undying passion to win. He constantly faced the challenge of igniting similar passion within the hearts of his team members. Woody once told a story about sensanation to a group of teenagers at Mike's church in Columbus, Ohio. Woody's story was so exciting, he stirred the desire in his audience to go out and play for Ohio State, even though they weren't football players. Stimulating creative desire is a true mark of a powerful leader. Woody told the young people:

"Before the Ohio State vs. Michigan game, I go down and tuck the youngsters (players) into bed at the hotel. I then return to campus and go over to the stadium where I stand in the middle of the football field on a bench.

"From this position, I play the entire game starting with the kickoff. I then go through every play, including the defense. From my vantage point, I simulate every touchdown and even hear the Ohio State Marching Band playing. I actually can feel the hard hits taken by our quarterback.

"From the middle of the football field, I smell the hot dogs and feel the fresh snow falling on my face. I live every moment. The blood rushes through my body, sending adrenaline coursing through my body. Ohio State always defeats Michigan by two touchdowns in my simulation."

Woody's sensanation starts with the sense of sight, then expands to employ the senses of sound, smell, taste and touch. As a rule, every one of us begins thinking in one of the senses and then begins accepting input from the other four. The initial sense is called the lead-off sense. In Woody's sensanation exercise, his lead-off sense was sight.

Proof by elimination

Scientific proof of how important our senses are—all our senses—is provided by sensory deprivation experiments such as sleep deprivation. These experiments have proven that deprivation of one or more of our senses can cause changes in personality and alterations in intellectual processes. Sensory deprivation exercises, called SDs, may be achieved by conducting vicarious experiences such as blindfolding a subject to simulate sightlessness. SDs heighten our sensitivity and open us to experience a wider-than-normal range of stimuli and empathetic responses.

Once one of the senses is taken away, our sensory systems immediately begin to compensate by heightening the awareness of the other senses. For example, testing has indicated that sightless people often have more highly developed senses of hearing and smell. The same holds true of hearing-impaired persons having heightened awareness to vibration, smell and other senses. Our minds and bodies depend more heavily on the constant inflow of sensory data than we are consciously aware of. Our minds gather, assess and respond to this never-ending flow of sensory information with amazing speed. Just blindfold yourself and see how fast you slow down.

The five senses: sound

Associations for hearing:

accent	babble	bang
bark	blare	blow
boom	burst	buzz
cackle	chatter	clang
clank	clap	clamor
clatter	clink	crash
creak	declare	detonate
din	earshot	echo
emit	explode	harmony
hum	intonation	jabber
jangle	jar	listen
loudness	melody	moan
modulation	murmur	music
noisy	note	outcry
racket	shout	

As with sight, the list could continue on and on. Let's go back to he solitary Woody Hayes perched on a bench in the middle of Ohio

Stadium the night before the Michigan game, hearing the Ohio State Marching Band, even though most of them were probably at home in bed at the time. The band, the crowd, the crashing of helmets and shoulder pads and the other sounds of an autumn Saturday afternoon on a college campus with a home game were each part of Woody's virtual football game. The sounds, audible only within his head, stirred his spirit and kindled his creative energies.

It would be hard to imagine a football game without the cacophony of a hyped-up marching band. Mike attended an NHL hockey game one night when the organ broke down. The hockey game just wasn't the same without the ceaseless staccato sounds from the electric organ. Imagine a baseball game without the organ. Music stirs the creative spirit and arouses the emotions. Our environments should never be without the appropriate music. Music lives in the so-called artistic right brain and helps us think out of the analytical left-brain box.

Although the concept is challenged by some, deprivation of sound is believed to have brought out an overcompensation factor in composer Ludwig von Beethoven; inventor, Thomas Edison; great thinker Buckminster Fuller; author Helen Keller and others. Living in a world without sound became a creative thinking tool to these people and others. We also can benefit immensely by regular periods of quiet time, meditation and contemplation.

We didn't fully appreciate true silence until we visited the sound elimination and test chamber at the General Electric factory in Louisville, Kentucky. Diane was game to try this out! After she entered the room, air was pumped out of a chamber surrounding the room to create a sound vacuum. It was an eerie experience, unnerving even. The silence was so complete, she could hear the sound of her own heart beating.

Being in an acoustic environment so silent helps us to appreciate the myriad of sounds we're subjected to even in the middle of the quietest night, in the midst of the quietest forest you can imagine.

We recommend the following exercise: Try sitting on the rim of the Grand Canyon at sunset, listening to Ferde Grofé's "Grand Canyon Suite" on your Walkman. After the sun goes down, remove your headset and sit in silence as the stars begin to appear. With the moonlight shining across the canyon walls, contemplate these phrases: *Be silent. Be still. Be aware.*

The five senses: taste

Taste determines flavor as we eat or drink. Associations include:

acid	aftertaste	bitter
chocolate	crave	delicious
drink	eat	flavor
fruity	garlic	ginger
hunger	juicy	libation
nibble	palate	piquancy
punch	relish	ripe
salty	sapidity	savor
sharp	sour	spicy
sweet	tang	tart
tasty	tasteless	thirst
tinge	unappetizing	unpalatable
unseasoned	vanilla	watered-down
zest	zing	zip

"You are what you eat" is a popular aphorism. It might be equally accurate to say, "What you are determines what you eat." Regardless of which statement you subscribe to, virtually everyone likes to eat, drink and be merry. Harsh diets do very little to improve our dispositions, though they may occasionally and temporarily decrease our size. Fasting might help monks and saints attain holy visions of angels and heavenly hosts, but most mere mortals drool for the secular, hedonistic delights of delicious hot fudge sundaes topped with nuts, whipped cream and a maraschino cherry.

During the filming of *Funny Girl*, Mike took Barbra Streisand on a private tour of Disneyland. Elliott Gould was also there. As they left the park, Mike asked Barbra what she enjoyed most about her visit. "The old-fashioned chocolate soda at New Orleans Square," she said. Mike recalls both she and Elliott had two! There's nothing like taste to trigger good feelings.

Tasting certain foods and drinking a favorite wine can unleash a wave of thoughts and memories that color current creative activities. (Of course, drinking too much wine can cause us to forget everything we just remembered!) Despite what bean counters and bottom-liners say, celebrating and socializing are important elements in the creative process. Walt Disney and Thomas Edison both made a habit of breaking bread with their teams. These incredibly creative men understood that some of the best ideas come out during informal social situations. Social events among working partners aren't always as history-making as the Last Supper, but the outcomes are usually more immediately positive.

In the competitive world we live in, there is an ever-increasing need for more originality and innovation. The call is for more creative solutions, more great ideas—but just try to get more money in the budget for celebrations, food and drink! The wingtippers, ball-bouncers, bottom-liners, pissers and moaners and pencil-pushers will scream out loud. Meanwhile, the same bunch will spend ridiculous amounts of money for a company jet that is totally unnecessary. It's pitiful.

> *"Socializing is a key element of the creative process;*
> *eating and drinking are part of the formula."*
>
> —Walt Disney

The five senses: touch

Associations for tactile activities:

arouse	blow	brush
caress	coarse	cold
contact	cuddling	dab
embrace	finger	fondling
grab	graze	handle
hard	hit	hot
hug	impact	kiss
lick	manipulate	massage
move	palpate	pat
pet	prickly	rough
shake	sharp	silky
smack	stroke	taste
textures	touchable	vibration

"Give me five!" This popular salutation employs touch to suggest approval, to convey congratulations, to say in a physical way, "all right" or "okay," and to symbolize bonding with another person. You could say it's an acceptable way we can stroke one another publicly.

We often joke that rather than fight with your accountants, stroke them instead. While this may seem odd, taboo even, our point is that touch often makes a more powerful communication bridge than mere words.

Like fasting, cold, reserved, uptight environments don't stir up much oil—pheromones are scent-related. Touch is a powerful form of recognition that unleashes creative energies within. We respond to soft and warm, silky and smooth, huggable and cuddly, big and firm—these touchy-feelies turn us on...or should turn us on.

Touching is one of the most stimulating of the physical senses. There is little creativity where people are not turned on physically, mentally and spiritually. Discovering areas of intellectual touching is one of the biggest mental turnons, and hearing a touching story is one of the biggest spiritual turnons possible. The laying on of hands and the washing of feet have long histories in sacred ceremonies because the touching involved deepens the experiences. (We don't mean to imply that we condone inappropriate touching in the workplace. In this day, sexual harassment is a legitimate issue. Any exploitation of physical contact, or even innocent gestures that could be misinterpreted, should be avoided and discouraged.)

Sexy bubbles

Bubble baths provide unique and potentially creative experiences that fall appropriately under the tactile category. Mike went for more than one year in Korea, during the war, without taking a real bath. He vowed that if he ever got out of there alive, he would take at least one bubble bath per day for the rest of his life. According to Mike, the only exception has been in some hotels that have thick sandpaper strips glued to the bottom of their tubs. You can't explain the marks they leave.

You might not believe sensual bubble baths are that important, but we're dead serious about how much bubble baths stimulate the creative thinking process. Bubble baths, good bubble baths, are an art form. We shouldn't just jump in the tub real quick like taking a shower. Bubble bath connoisseurs follow a proven ritual.

First, you must have lots of bubbles. In fact, the bubbles should be overflowing onto your bathroom floor. (When Mike was speaking at an Avon products convention, chairman Jim Preston and former senior vice president of corporate affairs Phyllis Davis sent us a case of Avon bubble bath!)

Candles placed around the tub add both romance and aroma to the experience, adding smell and sight to the soft touch of the warm soapy water. Your favorite music playing in the background and a glass of champagne, with fresh strawberries, complete the setting like in the movie *Pretty Woman*. After creating such a sensanation environment, it's a crime to enjoy it alone, but the rest is up to you.

"Cutaneous stimulation (touching) arouses creative urges."
—Dr. Ashley Montagu

The five senses: smell

Associations for perceiving and emitting odors:

air	aroma	bad breath
balm	bouquet	effluvium
essence	exhalation	fishy
fragrance	fresh air	incense
musk	odor	perfume
pungent	putrid	redolence
reek	savor	scent
scented	smell	smoky
sniff	snuff	spice
stench	stink	tang
trace	waft	whiff

The triggering effect of smells and odors on creativity is powerful. We often recall special aromas, even when we're not actually smelling them. Certain smells link up with our present thinking to form new responses. Certain smells conjure memories that link up with present thinking to form new responses.

Diane relishes the distinct smell and salty aroma of beautiful Crescent Beach on Siesta Key in Sarasota, Florida. She loves to walk for miles along that beach, breathing in the Gulf air and contemplating the sea—the same Gulf of Mexico that inspired Anne Morrow Lindbergh to write her best-selling *Gifts from the Sea.* John MacDonald wrote *Condominium* along the same stretch of beach.

Grantland Rice made his famous admonition "Stop and smell the roses" with this need to touch nature in mind. Smells easily reach us on an involuntary basis, but we rarely exercise our personal volition by actually picking up a rose, holding it, placing it near our nostrils and inhaling its delicate fragrance. Mike can remember the smell of his Grandmother Vance, who always ate apples. She comes to his mind every time Mike eats an apple or he's around someone eating an apple. Take every opportunity to introduce scents into your environments to enhance creativity.

Mark Vance, Mike's oldest son, introduced Mike to artificial aroma machines that produce a desired scent on command by inserting the right disk. The same principle applies to a more limited degree when viewing a video fish aquarium or fireplace. These gadgets are well and good as far as they go. However, nothing beats the real thing.

Tempting scents are all around you, even when you're not aware of them on a conscious level. Here are a few examples:

- Dave Hazen of Salem, Ohio, has a popcorn machine in the lobby of his insurance agency.
- Chili's restaurants serve sizzling fajitas to tempt your nostrils.
- When operations isn't hounding them for cost savings, airlines occasionally heat fresh chocolate chip cookies on board.
- Bill Marriott kept the lobby fireplace burning to greet guests at his hotels.

- Our friend, Marilyn Miglin, touches you with her sensational Pheromone brand perfume.
- The aroma of cappuccino captures you at the Buena Vista Cafe (Fisherman's Wharf, San Francisco).
- Women's magazines tempt you with perfume samplers.
- Your lover's scent that clings to you as a reminder of that last embrace fills you with warm thoughts—providing it wasn't garlic.

Smell opens your creativity to remembering and dreaming. A best kept secret of highly creative people is that they are lusty.

The five senses of Christmas

Nothing better exemplifies sensanation than Christmas season.

If you've heard of the Twelve Days of Christmas, then consider the five senses of Christmas. The sights, sounds, smells, tastes, and texture of the holiday season trigger childhood memories in virtually everyone. Memories, nostalgia, happiness, sadness, the feeling of family, loneliness, the desire to give gifts to those we love and those in need—all sweep over us—triggered by holiday season sensanation. Consider the following list of sensanation cues that make the holidays special:

Taste	Touch	Sight
plum pudding	prickly pine trees	wrapped presents
roast turkey	cold winds	garland
candy canes	Grandfather's lap	burning candles
mincemeat pie	kissing	falling snow
egg nog	Santa's cottony beard	mistletoe
fresh baked cookies	big hugs	tree lights glittering

Smell	Sound
evergreen trees	popping corn
burning logs	"Ho, ho, ho"
roasted chestnuts	wrapping paper crinkling
nutmeg	carols being sung
turkey cooking	busy stores
cinnamon	embers crackling in a fireplace

Working in color

We recommend that you always have a four-color pen handy, with red, blue, green and black ink. In the soundtrack to the Broadway musical *Barnum*, there's a memorable song called "The Colors of My Life." We recommend you pick up that soundtrack and listen to how the lyricist uses color as a metaphor for the life of colorful circus entrepreneur P.T. Barnum. Color is a marvelous dimension within the sight sense of the sensanation process.

Assuming you're not color-blind, if there is color within your range of vision it's going to affect you. Although virtually everyone appreciates the beauty color brings to their lives, most people still resist taking notes or working in anything but black or dark blue ink. It's time to break out of that limiting habit and become a rods-and-cones person. Use all the color that's available to you.

Do you recall your teachers saying things like, "This will be on the test"? If you had a four-color pen, you could have identified these important points in red!

We recommend to students and professionals alike that blue ink be used for assignments that are due or have a time line. Field trips, book reports, term papers, business expense reports, professional summaries, budgets, etc. can be noted in blue.

Some people respond better to the urgency of the red than the timeliness of the blue. Even if you're good at dealing with red-ink crisis, you must master the discipline and timing of the blue to truly rise to the top. If it's due, write it in blue.

Use the green ink for your private thoughts about something. Green is your participation color. Wherever green ink appears, you know that's where you've added your two-cents worth. Save the black ink for the main text of your notes. You can use more than the four colors named here, but use at least the black, blue, red and green colors to trigger the urgency or time commitment of your work.

In category note-taking, use red for the major points and black for the elaboration. In a competitive situation, when you have the tools to think out of the box and your competitor doesn't, you're three steps ahead because you have better methods.

Our team, working on the entrance complex to Walt Disney World, came up with a term for working with color called color lining. Walt, of course, was always interested in how color was going to be used. If you look at anything Disney, you immediately notice the imaginative use of color. They even go so far as to mix their own paint. A wonderful lady at the Disney studio named Grace Bailey developed some new techniques for mixing paint. That's how important it is for imaginative people to work with an unlimited color palette.

Creative tools for involvement

"[Humans] are tool-using animals. Without tools
[s]he is nothing, with tools [s]he is all."
—Thomas Carlyle

The information age has made the acquisition of knowledge— learning—the Zeitgeist of our time. If you wish to succeed, or remain successful, you must be a student for a lifetime. Although many people give lip service to the notion of lifelong learning, continuing education is the fundamental strategy—both personally and professionally— which enables us to think out of the box.

This emphasis on learning presents a formidable challenge to every parent, teacher and leader. The understanding that knowledge is power has made education and training booming industries. Buckminster Fuller told Diane and Mike at dinner that we're now living in a "Mind Quake!" We're both fascinated by the way Bucky's term captures the explosive growth of information and knowledge taking place around us at any given time.

There is a potential problem with this new emphasis. Most students don't learn how to be true students during the formative educational years of their lives. Instead, they learn to cram for the exam instead of taking in the mind-expanding educational experience. This carries over into ineffective leadership styles when crisis occurs. True students, like effective leaders, are rare commodities.

Tricks of the trade

Now that we've had a glimpse at category note-taking, sensanation and working in color, it's important to better understand the new age we're living in that makes such tools necessary. Creative thinking is becoming a modern trade of the information age. Every trade has unique tools that are created for specific purposes. Success in any trade requires skilled use of the tools. Creative thinking underscores the need to take an extra step by creating yet more tools.

There is a plethora of instruments in the creative thinking toolbox. Yet, the three tools focused on to this point are especially useful because they tend to work universally. Our friend Steve Pfaff says, "Find me something that really works—that would be original." Not only do category note-taking, sensanation and working in color really work, they're simple to use and can be easily taught in a short period of time. Most important, they get the user involved.

Brain showers

"I can't tell you much about my past, but my future is spotless."
—Jim Newton, author of *Uncommon Friends*

Jim Newton's humorous but sage remark makes a cogent point underscoring the importance of starting off with a clean sheet of paper, especially when we're engaged in creative thinking. We need to ensure a spotless future by clearing up our thinking. We must make a conscious effort to clear the table, push the erase button, and start out fresh if we hope to arrive at new and different solutions.

Most of us drag so much old baggage around it's a wonder we get anywhere at all. Old baggage binds us to predrawn conclusions and obstacles that block innovative ideas. What we need are some brain showers. Mike's son, John Vance, introduced his dad to his creative solution for handling a bad day. He told Mike he took brain showers.

"What on earth is a brain shower?" Mike asked John with considerable intrigue.

John replied, "Sometimes when I'm sad or upset about something that's happened to me, Dad, I stand in the shower and let hot water run down over my head for a long time."

By now, John had Mike completely hooked. Mike pressed him further. "What does that accomplish?"

Without missing a beat, John said, "The water washes out the old thoughts and then I can put some new thoughts in my head."

John conversed about his idea with ease, as if Mike should have been readily able to understand such an obvious solution. He fully understood his brain shower ritual was symbolic. Nevertheless, it was meaningful to him and had all the elements of a child's unadulterated approach to a cleansing process. Adults often don't get around to such creative solutions. Consequently, we get psychosclerosis—a hardening of the mind.

Diane and Mike had a chance encounter at the Los Angeles International Airport with the distinguished philosopher and writer Dr. Mortimer Adler. Dr. Adler is an enormous intellect who was having a tough day enduring the vicissitudes of traveling. Mike shared the story of John's brain shower technique with Dr. Adler, hoping it might ease his burden, or at least distract him momentarily from his troubles.

"What a delightful idea," Dr. Adler exclaimed in his inimitable manner. "What I need is a good brain shower!" Dr. Adler understood: Creative thought requires a clear head—free from cobwebs.

Mike lived through a dramatic incident on a troop ship bringing him back from combat duty in Korea (1951), which revealed the importance that clean slate is to the creative thinking process. There were hundreds of American soldiers on board for the crossing, many of whom were World War II veterans. It's safe to say that every combat troop on board had seen enough war to last forever. Mike and the others were sick and tired of anything and everything that reminded them of that horrific time in their lives. They needed to get away from the sensanation of war, in every sense of the word.

Mike was standing on the ship's stern one evening, watching the sea gulls that seemed to be following them back to California. The gulls were flying just above the white spume caused by the ship's giant wake. Mike recalls daydreaming about cruising under the Golden Gate Bridge into beautiful San Francisco Bay, fantasizing about the first things he would do when he landed stateside and wishing at the same time that the ship would go faster and get him and the other soldiers home sooner.

Noticing an object floating in the foam, drifting out of sight into the vastness of the sea, Mike couldn't make it out in the twilight. Then he saw another object, just like the other one. Then another and another. They were articles of clothing—shoes, socks, shirts, coats, undershorts. There were other objects, too: boxes, cans, canteens, mess gear and even a wardrobe trunk.

The soldiers were throwing overboard the remains of the war—Korean flotsam and jetsam being consumed by the Pacific Ocean. This was more than a brain shower. This was an emotional deluge, a purging of personal histories, the evidence sinking into the sea forever, taking with it, hopefully, the memories of war. The haunting ritual continued during the remainder of Mike's voyage back to the states. He joined in the therapy with the other soldiers, tossing out the memories from his duffel bag. It was nearly empty by the time his ship docked in San Francisco.

Mike and his shipmates were trying to achieve a fresh start. They wanted desperately to have a spotless future in front of them because so much of the past was dark and cloudy. They were ready to live a normal life again and establish something, anything, to escape the regimentation of the military. Mike said he and the others thanked God that they were among the lucky ones who made it back. Many had missing limbs, blinded eyes or a piece of shrapnel embedded forever somewhere in their bodies.

Mike never again experienced anything similar to these feelings as he returned to the United States from Korea. Then he saw her, standing on the dock.

A beautiful young woman whose husband had been killed during the early days of the Korean conflict. She met every incoming troop ship and stood on the dock singing "God Bless America," just like Kate Smith did or Whitney Houston might. The soldiers cried, they laughed, they screamed with joy listening to her sing her heart out. Mike and his buddies were home again!

Experiences of our past, like the berthing of the ship, produce the kind of passions that ignite the flames of creative thought. To return home again, you have to have been somewhere. To have passion, you must want something desperately.

Genuine passion is the fuel for creativity.
The tools and passion are yours.
It's time to think out of the box!

Thomas Edison: Inspired

Thomas Alva Edison is the only person on our list of nine out-of-the-box thinkers that neither one of us had ever known personally. Our best information on Edison came through Jim Newton of Fort Myers, Florida, the man who parts traffic like Moses parted the Red Sea. As described earlier, our long-time friends Danny and Theo Cox introduced us to Jim and Ellie Newton during a visit to the Edison home and museum. Jim's stimulating book, *Uncommon Friends,* is the powerful story of his friendship and sometimes working relationship with Edison, Henry Ford, Harvey Firestone, Charles Lindbergh and Dr. Alexis Carrel. As a young man, Jim met and became friends with this circle of intellectuals and his insight into their lives is authentic and remarkable. Jim, now 90, developed Edison Park in Fort Myers while he was still in his 20s. He was treated much like a son by Mina and Thomas Edison.

In 1994, Jim recounted for us a few of the most basic attributes of the great inventor: Edison was granted 1,093 patents.[1] He was the father of modern research and development, the light bulb, the phonograph, talking motion pictures—and, most interestingly, the concept of scientific teamwork. His laboratories were among the first to promote collaboration among scientists and were known to be the first industrial research labs and facilities. He was also nearly stone deaf, which made collaborative

---

[1]Thomas Edison was granted a new patent on the average of every 10 to 12 days. Many of his medical and philanthropic developments, however, were never patented but made available to all mankind immediately.

efforts more challenging. Further, he was known as a great humanitarian and the poet of technology.

Jim told us that Edison was strictly a team person, rejecting the suggestion made by some that he worked only in isolation. According to Newton, Edison always involved those around him. Edison himself said:

> *"People sometimes talk of me as a lone inventor. Nonsense!*
> *Where would I have been without Charles Batchelor,*
> *Steinmitz, Jack Kuesi and all the others?"*

> *"You never saw such a mixed crew as we had at Menlo Park.*
> *We all worked as a team."*

The famous inventor had a tenacious temperament stemming from childhood experiments in chemistry. He wouldn't give up simply because he experienced failure. After a thousand failures in trying to develop the incandescent light bulb, Edison tossed it off by saying "We're making progress."

Sarasota summit

We invited Jim Newton to what we called the 1994 Siesta Key summit in Sarasota, Florida, at Mike's house, on the subjects of creativity and Thomas Edison. We spent hours seated at the gathering table in Mike's Kitchen for the Mind™[2] talking about Edison and Henry Ford. It was a memorable powwow. Jim's firsthand knowledge and deep understanding of Edison's genius led us to explore the creative techniques he used in his laboratories. Jim gave us some direct Edison quotes. We carefully copied down the quotes, and often reflect on their meaning.

> *"The answer is out there if you will look for it.*
> *Never, never stop the search."*

> *"The secret of staying afloat in business is to create*
> *something people will pay for."*

---

[2]The Kitchen for the Mind™ is a creativity-stimulating Team Center in the home. You and your family don't leave your brains at the office or at school. Creativity is a never-ending process. You'll read more about these kitchens later.

"The greatest invention in the world is the mind of a child."

Picking up on Edison's sensitivity and optimism, Jim Newton signs off his letters: "The Best Is Yet to Be." Jim and Ellie Newton are fantastic models of what we should all aspire to. Their enthusiasm and zeal for life carries them through their mature years, not as observers, but as active participants in the world around them. While strolling around the grounds of the Edison house in Fort Myers, Jim paused at the entrance to Edison's long boat dock.

"Edison would come out here nearly every morning while in Fort Myers and sit at the end of the dock, which stretched out into the bay, holding a fishing pole, dangling the line in the water. But he never had any bait on the hook."

Thomas Edison confessed to exploiting the protocol of fishermen when he admitted to Jim: "I fish with no bait because then no one bothers me, neither fish nor man."

Jim called Edison's form of meditation "cosmic fishing." (We asked our designer Larry Broedow to sketch a picture of Edison doing "cosmic fishing" as a gift.) Jim figures he was fishing for ideas out in the river. We figure there's a timeless lesson for everyone in the cosmic fishing story. Creativity can be found at the end of a fishing pole if your line is in the water and you never stop searching, as our friend Steve Pfaff says. Thomas Edison knew the importance of working in collaboration with others and meditating alone.

Even though Thomas Edison was the only one of our nine human models neither one of us knew personally, thanks to Theo and Danny Cox and Jim and Ellie Newton, we feel as if we've experienced the essence of the man. He inspires us to this day and will inspire students of creativity for probably the rest of time. Thomas Edison's best practices include:

- Experimentation.
- Research.
- Maintaining notebooks.
- Teamwork.
- Personal meditation and reflection.
- Crediting others.
- Tenacity.

CHAPTER 3

The nine-point formula for success

$$\frac{I^3 + P^3}{V + M} = C^3$$

The nine-point formula for success has gradually emerged from our experiences with diverse clients around the world, as well as from highly creative individuals from nearly every profession. Although cryptic at first glance, the formula has proven to be valid through application and implementation on the firing line. And, by the end of this chapter, it will become clear and meaningful to you.

We are constantly engaged in projects with companies to cultivate their cultures. Helping companies transform their present cultures into creative cultures is a constant theme at the Creative Thinking Association and is one of our main business activities.

Jack Welch, General Electric's chairman, encouraged Mike when he was working with them, "Get it in a book!" Therefore, the formula we're about to describe has a long and successful history rooted in creative consulting assignments, cultural transformation, team building, patent development and design projects we have led over the years. Each one of the nine formula elements have been applied in projects with our clients including General Electric, Johnson & Johnson, Owens Corning Fiberglas, AT&T, Apple Computer, Entergy, Motorola, Glaxo Pharmaceutica and others.

Failures in business and personal life often occur when people scatter their shots too far. We instinctively understand that without focus or direction, energy, talent and ability become diluted. The most effective people know the value of concentrating their resources on well-defined goals and objectives. Although most people understand this principle, they still fail to aim their efforts at two or three main objectives. The formula for success is designed to help users stay on target.

Individuals and organizations frequently attempt more than they can do because they fail to comprehend the big picture or grand design behind a project. The perspective gained from understanding and appreciating the big picture enables us to identify and concentrate on the specifics required to successfully accomplish the many tasks that need to be done. The Walt Disney World main entrance complex team was an excellent example of a team that constantly kept in focus the big picture and maintained that perspective in designing even down to the finest details of the project. Regularly standing back and asking "What's unique about this project?" provides the perspective you're looking for.

The practice of narrowing your field of focus is called "delimiting the scope of inquiry." The formula for success was developed to concentrate our creativity, resources and energies on just those tasks that must be done in order to succeed. The delimiting process helps us avoid wasting valuable time, energy and resources. We refer to those specific components of a successful project as imperatives.

The formula is further correlated with business and cultural trillitrends,[1] which are fast becoming the guiding principles, assumptions and beliefs for the remainder of this century and into the next millennium.

---

[1]Really big trends.

Emerging technologies also correlate with these trends. The formula itself is comprised of three elements that also are the desired end results:

$$\underline{C^3}$$

Caring

Cooperating

Creating

We begin our discussion of the nine-point formula with the end results, which are caring, cooperating and creating. (The first part of the formula will be discussed later.)

Caring

"If you want someone to care, capture their minds and their hearts."

—Roy O. Disney

Roy Disney made that statement to Mike one day, observing the crowds, as they walked through Disneyland together. He understood that the spirit of a caring person is respected around the world as one of the most desirable human qualities. It's a quality no longer reserved for "do-gooders" or social fanatics. Finding solutions to the myriad of social problems facing the world today requires a genuine caring attitude among people striving to change the status quo.

A caring attitude was once considered to be "soft." We now know "soft" is truly hard. By hard, we're acknowledging that the most important goals are usually the hardest to achieve. Diane, in her continuing work with corporate clients worldwide, is cognizant that caring is most often the missing link in organizational or cultural change. Apparently, some people don't feel it's important, or perhaps the thought of caring intimidates them. Whatever the reason, we can't emphasize enough how critical it is to incorporate caring into actual practice.

Those who genuinely care are highly sensitive to human needs, observing what should be done to correct problems while being guided by passion, dedication, commitment and the will to persevere. Tenacity to do the difficult comes from feeling a deep concern for humanity's ills as well as humanity's promise. Margaret (Peg) Cushman, who has spent a lifetime in the nursing profession, has emphasized the importance of caring in her leadership with visiting nurses. She presents gold-star pins to her nursing associates for recognition of exemplary acts of caring. Our good friends, Val and Bill Halamandaris, started a much needed organization called The Caring Institute in Washington, D.C., to help recognize people and stimulate the caring spirit within them.

The Caring Institute presents annual Caring Awards to individuals who display caring attitudes in exemplary ways. Val and Bill deserve high praise for their unique social entrepreneurship, which increases awareness of this meritorious quality within the human character. At our annual Creativity Celebration, recognizing and honoring those who have made significant contributions to the pursuit of creativity, the Creative Thinking Association of America presented Val and Bill with its highest award in recognition of their efforts in founding The Caring Institute.

"To be or not to be" is "to care or not to care." The feeling of being a worthwhile person and self-esteem in general are rooted in authentic concern for seeking solutions to the most disturbing and troublesome problems. As Roy Disney pointed out to Mike, the world needs to capture more minds and hearts in the habit of caring.

Those who care see what needs to be done.
Caring replaces indifference.
Motivation is a byproduct of caring.

Cooperating

"Weed out the bureaucracies that stifle cooperation and collaboration."
—Jack Welch, Chairman, General Electric

The monumental leadership transformation taking place has introduced a more collaborative effort. Team-based leadership is the direct result of transformation in the workplace. There is so much knowledge and information available today about what should be done to prosper that no one person is smart enough to act in isolation. It's more than just a desire for collaborative work habits—we need each other.

This exponentially expanding reservoir of knowledge coupled with increasing interdependence is a paradox. On one hand, technology has made it possible for a single individual to accomplish extraordinary tasks. Simultaneously, much of the same technology has made it both possible and highly desirable to network with one another, adding our contributions to the contribution of others through job-sharing and creative means.

As working together becomes more and more desirable, a spirit of cooperation becomes increasingly necessary. Although you might work in physical isolation, the tools and resources you use were developed by others. You're no doubt in constant communication with others through the use of advanced technology. The bottom line is, we're never really alone anymore. Even working in physical isolation requires some degree of cooperation. Living with a partner requires a much greater and immediate degree of cooperation. Either way, not being cooperative has become synonymous with having an "attitude."

Those with "attitude" aren't considered good team players. No matter what you do, cooperation and interaction with other humans and increasingly sophisticated technology is essential to success.

Cooperators are among the long-term survivors.
Predators move toward extinction.
Cooperative behavior creates strength and success.
Collaborative leadership style requires cooperation.

Creating

Creativity is the making of the new and
the rearranging of the old in a new way.

Over the years, productivity and quality have been driving forces in business. However, creativity and thinking out of the box are overtaking these traditional motivators as the new engines powering competitive ability in the global marketplace. We founded the Creative Thinking Association of America specifically to enhance, encourage and share great creative thought. We felt the time had come for creativity and the art of creating to receive rightful recognition as one of the major thrusts in life. The Association promotes awareness of the importance of creativity, and helps to stimulate it.

The same old solutions just aren't working anymore. People quickly get tired of sequels, copies and phonies. A place where there is no excitement or anticipation about the next great gadget, invention or source of entertainment would be a dull, lifeless community—a consumer wasteland. Who could imagine life without:

- The original Ford Mustang.
- Television.
- Stereo FM.
- Panavision.
- The automatic washer/dryer.
- The personal computer.
- Wash-and-wear fabrics.
- Jet travel.
- Cellular telephones.
- Fax machines.
- Hair dryers.
- Home video/VCRs.

"Bring on those products," demands the consumer. "Create something for me." Are you answering the call to creativity? When Walt Disney was urged to make a sequel to the hugely successful *Three Little Pigs* animated motion picture, he said, "No more pigs! You can't top pigs with pigs." He didn't see any creativity in repetition. Sameness and boredom are the opposite of creativity. (Walt ultimately gave in to the pressure from his associates and allowed them to make a *Three Little Pigs* sequel. It bombed.)

Invention, innovation and originality are the lifeblood of any company, organization or government. This might not mean inventing new products as much as it might mean inventing new ways to market them.

It might not be as important for you to have the newest gadget as it is to have the most innovative gadget. Some companies have built their entire success around an identity based on originality. Disney is an excellent example of a company from whom consumers have come to expect originality, along with invention, innovation and good family values. Once you've done pigs, move on.

Invention, innovation and originality are rooted in the fertile soil of creativity, making creativity in research and development the foundation for long-term survival. Cures have yet to be found for diseases such as AIDS. We must discover methods of controlling plagues and insects and bacteria. Everywhere you look—from transportation to lodging, from medicine to motion pictures, from social needs to recreation, from communications to education—the challenge to create new and better ways never ends.

Creativity is the thrust of life.
We need new and original products.
The urge to create will be satisfied.
We're getting more and more copies and fewer and fewer originals.

The C³ (caring, cooperation, creating) components of the formula for success can appear superficial. Taken only at face value, they *are* superficial. It's only when you personalize them that they become indispensable. Caring accomplishes nothing until you and your organization are involved. No one can truthfully claim they wouldn't benefit from a more caring environment. Such an environment would add significantly to the bottom line of virtually any organization.

Cooperating benefits individuals and organizations in much the same way. Yet, it must become yours. You must take responsibility and ownership for cooperating and making it meaningful to you and your circumstances. Cooperation might wear one face in organization A and another face in organization B. The overall definition is the same. But what cooperation means to specific people, given their specific environment and activities, can be very different.

Creativity is especially personal. Individual people as well as entire organizations take on an identity based on their commitment to creativity. It may be subtle and understated, but the degree to which we allow creativity to enrich our lives will rub off on those around us. Creativity is anything but superficial. It represents the very core of who we are and why we do what we do. If we have problems with what we or our organization are doing or the results we're getting, the solution, whatever it might be, calls for creativity.

If cynics wag their heads at the notion of caring, cooperation and creativity, it's only because they haven't been to the mountaintop. They haven't seen either the tremendous, life-changing benefits of the three C's or the immense need people have for each one of them. Human experience is the most compelling evidence in favor of caring, cooperation and creativity. They're considered admirable traits because they improve the quality of people's lives.

To put it another, perhaps more direct way: Without establishing a foundation of genuine caring, cooperation and creativity, the rest of the success formula will have nothing to stand on. If this sounds like we're preaching a sermon here, we are—because we've tried to live the three C's in our own lives. In many ways—some of which we'll describe as we go along—caring, cooperating and creativity brought us the enrichment we enjoy today. The three C's are the paving stones on anyone's road to success. Without them, you have nothing to stand on. People do try shortcuts to success. But they often fail.

Facing reality

You can't make someone a caring person by simply saying, "You should care more."

Despite the hype, even the most convincing motivational encounters fail to produce the passion necessary to sustain a long-term commitment to caring. Minds and hearts are only transformed through consistent, trust-building experience.

By the same thinking, someone can't be commanded to be cooperative. A command might produce obedient behavior, albeit temporary, but there's still no inner motivation to make someone a team player. Without a true desire to be part of a collaborative effort or a cooperative spirit, a collaborative atmosphere is impossible.

As often as we continue to wave a magic wand over someone's head (called a motivational seminar) and saying, "You will create," it still won't produce a creative person. There's no way to unleash the urge to create until someone personally feels the need and sees a vision of what is possible. The actual act of creating something is inexorably tied to motivation.

Consequently, developing all three of these qualities—caring, cooperation, creativity—must be correlated with the methods to achieve them within the reality of human behavior. They have to become real and meaningful rather than superficial. They must be doable rather than theoretical. One of the many ways Walt Disney amazed the world was by not only dreaming big dreams, but by dreaming doable dreams.

Think of C^3 as a mission. Once you believe they're worthwhile and attainable goals, you're ready to establish the methods to make them a reality. The next step is to put the cause behind the desired effect C^3 is designed to achieve.

Preceding C^3 in the formula for success are the corresponding methods known as I^3:

$$\underline{I^3}$$

Involved

Informed

Inspired

Involved people care

Involvement is the primary method for inculcating a caring attitude into our character. When you want to develop the positive attributes of a caring person, such as passion, commitment, tenacity and dedication, the secret is to get the person or persons involved. It isn't enough to try and make people feel part of something, they must really become part of something.

You can watch the game on television, from the stands or from the sidelines. But you can't claim to be fully involved until you're in the contest, playing. One of the most important truths Mike learned from Walt and Roy Disney is that people want to be involved. If they're not involved, it's due to some unnatural and prohibitive factor. People naturally want to make a contribution. They want to be players, participants and part of the group. Being involved fulfills the human desire to be included. Involvement produces a sense of belonging. Voyeurism can never measure up to the experience of doing it yourself.

Caring is a byproduct of the foundational type of involvement or at least one that meaningful relationships are built on. One-night stands, quickie relationships and drive-by associations, fun though they might be, characteristically don't result in commitment and long-term dedication. Participatory styles of leading and organizing people have evolved from the increasing demand for teamwork. Genuine involvement is popular not only because of the natural desire for belonging, but because increased involvement pays off with increased results. Caring and involvement are natural companions.

If you want people to care, get them involved.
People want to get into the act—let them.
Adopt a participative style to involve people.
Technology makes it possible to participate and
communicate without a hierarchy or go-betweens.

Informed people cooperate

Norman Brinker, the famed restaurateur whose profile you've read, said, "You have to know something in order to do something." Knowledge, skills and competence can only be developed when people are informed. Even though someone can be ordered to cooperate, he or she can't truly be forced to cooperate. People acting against their will usually wind up resisting leadership and/or faking a cooperative attitude. On the bright side, those who are truly involved in the process and informed about what's going on in the organization are motivated to cooperate. The motivational factors necessary for a collaborative effort fall into place more easily when people are kept well-informed.

Action without information is usually irresponsible. We hear constant complaining from prospective clients who say, "We never implement anything around here. Our company divides people into teams, we announce that we're empowering people—but nothing we recommend is ever done. We're out of the loop and in the dark because we lack information about what's really going on in our own company."

The value of information works in every direction, top to bottom, bottom to top, inside out and outside in. There's a common ranking of information that characterizes the data like this:

1. Nice to know.
2. Need to know.
3. Absolutely, positively need to know.

For people to be usefully informed, they need access to all three levels. Knowledge of "nice to know" information, while not essential, makes people feel included. Withholding any type of information can break the spirit of a team. Informed people have the facts to act on and the knowledge to be successful.

> *People in the dark are rarely cooperative.*
> *Being informed is essential before taking action.*
> *When people know what's going on,*
> *they're much more likely to cooperate.*

Inspired people create

Some people just seem to have it. And some people who have it seem to have a lot more of it than others. What is it, anyway? Good looks? Charisma? Presence, class, stature, reputation, sex appeal? Each of these characteristics are part of it. However, the ability to inspire others goes far beyond just having it.

We tend to be most inspired by people who achieve noteworthy success and accomplish worthwhile objectives with their lives on behalf of others. We're especially inspired by those who overcome obstacles and serious hardships. Our spirits are uplifted when someone does something to make life better and happier for everyone. True inspiration results from an active accomplishment, creating something new or revitalizing something old, that directly or indirectly benefits us.

Inspired leadership is applauded and often rewarded with some combination of recognition, money, prizes, influence, affection and social immortality. Yet, inspired leadership isn't a course offered at business schools. I've never seen "inspired leadership" listed on a person's resume as a major asset. Nevertheless, inspiration is the primary challenge for every leader because it's one of the ingredients for creativity, and vice versa.

We stress the connection between inspiration and creativity and recommend designing and implementing these interdependent qualities into your organization as you continue reading. When we say that inspirational leadership is a weak or altogether missing link in organizations, we speak from experience. Analyzing the work we do to help organizations grow and develop, it's clear that we work the hardest at assisting leaders in how to inspire and motivate their people and themselves.

Clients come to us with the expectations that we'll talk to their people and motivate them. They usually realize that they're asking us to be examples in the area of inspiration. As we work with companies, large and small, we occasionally see examples of fantastic leadership. Too often we see people in corporate leadership positions who are competent as strategic planners, but can't inspire. Their employees are hungry for examples to follow.

Often, leadership-challenged management hires consultants to do their work for them. But, unless the consultant includes methods to teach the art and meaning of inspirational leadership, company funding is wasted. It's the old saying about teaching someone to fish. Motivational speakers can be like an overdose of caffeine—you get wired for a short time, then you need another cup. The answer is not for a company to hire a motivational speaker every time to pump up people.

It's a far wiser and more productive investment for everyone in your organization, from the top down, to learn the craft of creativity. You must make it a priority to nurture and develop inspirational leaders throughout your organization. Creativity begets inspiration and vise versa. In a creative environment, filled with challenge and true rewards, people become naturally inspired. A corporate executive worried about the motivational wasteland in his or her organization needs to think about a concept we mentioned a moment ago:

Inspiration is the byproduct of active accomplishment.

Active accomplishments mostly take place in creative environments. Learning to lead with inspiration doesn't necessarily mean buying into motivational hype. Becoming an inspirational leader means leading your people on a journey of discovery by charting a creative course where they also learn how to self-motivate.

Creativity thrives where people are inspired. Inspiration is a nearly forgotten leadership skill—a weak or even missing link in organizational life. Creativity and inspiration chase each other around a self-renewing cycle. We are inspired by the things we create, just as being inspired causes us to think out of the box!

Making C^3 (caring, cooperating, creativity) fully work for us requires the *final* component of the nine-point formula—P^3.

$$\underline{\text{P}^3}$$
People
Place
Product

People

"People cause and experience problems when they lack the skills to succeed in the environment in which they've been placed."
—Walt Disney

Training and development have become increasingly important priorities in organizations because informed and educated people tend to be cooperative people. It pleases us to hear the concept of a learning organization discussed more and more frequently during our travels around the world. Since Mike was appointed Dean of the Disney University and put in charge of people development at the corporate level, the training programs he's developed and the work he's done with organizations continue to underscore the importance of learning organizations. Few people we've known or worked with could use the team concept within a learning organization to focus people's ideas and energies better than the Disney brothers.

Turning Walt's quotation inside out reveals the importance of training and developing people in your organization:

> *People contribute and successfully solve problems*
> *when they have developed the skills to succeed in the*
> *environment in which they have been placed.*

Most companies we encounter know the importance of training and developing their people, but because they don't invest an adequate amount of financial or human resources to back up their professional beliefs, it becomes just more lip service. When we press them on the issue, they admit that, to them, the training and development of their people is the "soft stuff." Fortunately, many of them are now beginning to appreciate how essential and critical people development is to survival. If they're not convinced when they first meet us, they usually are converts by the time we've finished working with them. We continue to stress the importance of training and accommodating change in the organization.

When Mike asked Card Walker, later president and CEO of Walt Disney Productions, what his training OD budget was, Card said, "Spend what's required, because we'll get it back tenfold." Bean counters cringe when they hear comments like that! When we encounter an executive with a strong belief in the value of well-trained, highly skilled and educated people, we go out and have a celebration at the nearest bar. Card Walker was that kind of man you celebrate over.

At the Disney University, we developed a catalog of available courses so those who wanted a long and successful Disney career could plan their company education. To this day, we are still helping companies set up their own universities. We're not talking about orientation programs of "feel-good" experiences. We help company universities offer a broad range of world-class learning opportunities by teaching them how to access cybernation resources, the information superhighway and a multitude of other available tools. Too many training and human resource specialists devote their time and money to dreaming up clever multimedia productions instead of planning training that is visionary.

Place

"We have very few inferior people in the world. We have lots
of inferior environments. Try to enrich your environment."
— Frank Lloyd Wright

Your place is your environment and your challenge is to enrich your environment as much as possible. If you are a leader, your challenge includes enriching the environment of the people you lead. We're not talking exclusively about your work environment. We're talking about the environment in which you live. That includes your home environment and the home environment of everyone in your organization. We and anyone we influence should live and work in enriched places.

Small companies often start out by creating a Team Center, which doubles also as their learning center. We help them design the most creative environments possible to access the training and development resources we've enumerated. Larger companies with larger, better-established training and development operations establish Team Centers to add the value of a creative environment to their development of people and products.

Because helping clients design creative environments is a major emphasis in our work, we've devoted more discussion to the issues of place and environment in Chapter 5.

Product

*"You can't change anything by fighting or resisting it. You change
something by making it obsolete through superior methods."*
— Buckminster Fuller

For many organizations, service is their product. But just talking
about a product or service won't change it. The creation of prototypes,
models and services begins the change process. As we see a need,
problem or opportunity, we move to address it. The more successful we
are at creating solutions to fill the need, resolve the problem and
embrace the opportunity, the more inspired we become. The development of new products and services, or the improvement of existing
ones, calls for inspired people who know how to think out of the box!
Creation of original product happens when skilled people live and
work in creative environments.

You've been introduced to the nine pieces of the formula for success. The next ingredient is to incorporate vision and methods to make
the formula produce the caring, cooperation and creativity we seek.

V + M   Vision and Method

Our vision is an expression of our goals, dreams and objectives. It is
what we want to do or accomplish. Our method is an expression of how
we are going to do it. The method should be intrinsic in the vision.

The necessary vision and its intrinsic methods are described in the
next chapters as we deal with what's keeping some of us in the box.

Louis L'Amour: Involved

By 1964, a variety of intriguing guests had appeared on Mike's television show, "Men at the Top," on KNBC and KTLA in Los Angeles. The show's purpose was to broaden the horizons for viewers who were interested in learning basic elements of success and the true nature of creativity. We've learned that people who achieve notable heights usually consider the principles of their success to be very simple and basic, even though the nuances can be complex and intricate upon closer examination.

Among Mike's favorite guests was the prolific author of Western novels, Louis L'Amour. At the time, L'Amour had more than 100 books in print, with sales of over 200 million copies. To Mike, Louis L'Amour was creativity personified. He was also one of the most ingratiating people you could have ever met. It was difficult not to admire this man, as do millions of readers of his exciting adventures.

The KTLA studio in Los Angeles was transformed into a different environment when the dynamic author walked onto the set. The crew and technicians, usually blasé about even the biggest celebrities, were genuinely excited to meet him. KTLA employees who weren't even working on the show crowded into the control room to watch him.

Louis was a consummate raconteur who had the ability to raise the dead with his colorful tales of wondrous adventures. His contagious spirit got in your blood. In fact, L'Amour's energy and enthusiasm sort of stuck to you after spending time with him.

*"We can not learn anything about experiences
we've never had. Our creations come from our
experiences—both real and those we've read about."*

You could expect a celebrated author to equate reading with a real-life experience. And why not? Reading and storytelling are how we learn the most about life. People generally know numerous facts and tall tales about the Civil War, although they didn't live during this historical period. So L'Amour's point is well-taken. What we do with our experiences is mostly of our own choosing.

Louis told the television audience:

"If you want to be creative, go where your questions lead you. Do things. Have a wide variety of experiences and take field trips to distant places. Reach outside of your everyday sphere of influence; it keeps you from being too provincial.

"We can't learn anything from experiences we've never had. Life is too long not to do it right, not to participate—we end up dying before we live. There's a lot of seconds between birth and death when you've withdrawn from the game. To die before we live is agonizing.

"Life is too long not to do it right."

The one-hour show went by in what seemed like five minutes as L'Amour explained how he wrote his books. He was rushed by nearly everyone in the studio the moment we finished taping the program. It seemed to everyone as if they were coming face-to-face with a character right out of one of his novels.

Louis L'Amour and his wife had lunch one day with Mike in the Coral Room (the executive dining room at the Disney Studio). Walt Disney, Fred MacMurray, Greer Garson and other luminaries were also having lunch in the Coral Room. But none seemed to stand out like Louis and his beautiful wife. This was a red-letter day during which Mike asked Louis how he cultivated his personal creativity. "Read, read, read—do, do, do," came the answer. L'Amour went on, "Reading is a form of doing and doing makes you want to read."

Mike asked Louis why he placed such a strong emphasis on reading as related to creativity. L'Amour told him: "Reading is like a fantastic time machine. You can go anywhere, any time, and become anyone you want to be without moving from your chair. Reading is magic! It inspires creativity and imagination. I can't imagine life without reading."

Mike asked him for another practice to stimulate creativity.

"Listening," L'Amour said instantly. "Be sure to listen carefully. Listen to what people are saying because you can learn a great deal. Too many people hear but never truly listen. Experience life, read about life and listen to life."

He quoted his novel *Mustang Man*: "There's no way I know of that a body can foresee the future, but sometimes he can read it pretty well if he knows what folks think."

After lunch, the two men went to Mike's office, where Mike showed Louis the secret wall behind the curtain. He remarked, "You should add another truth to your wall about creativity. Creativity is inflamed by sex, passion and desire. Passion comes from being involved in life's challenges, joys and sorrows. It stimulates a desire to take action."

We've seen that last comment proven over and over again working and talking with people and organizations all over the globe. Louis L'Amour's best practices included:

- Avid reading.
- Prolific writing.
- Passion for adventure.
- Living and loving.
- Experiencing triumph and tragedy.
- Listening.

CHAPTER 4

The monumental transformation

"You can't learn anything from experiences you're not having."
—Louis L'Amour

The following thoughts are based in part on remarks Mike made during his keynote address to the American Institute of Architects (AIA) at its national convention in Los Angeles. As people who focus their talents and energies on space design, architects are keenly aware of the impact that environment has on our personal and professional lives. You might also think of yourself metaphorically as an architect. When you think of your organization or your home, picture the environment the way an architect would. The first emotion you should experience is the empowering feeling that you are the master of your immediate environment. You help create it, build it and change it as necessary to meet your needs.

There is a monumental transformation taking place in how we work, how we live and how we organize ourselves and our environment. The change is so gigantic that many people feel intimidated and choose to deny rather than face it. Nothing will ever be the same again. To say a new day has dawned might sound like a cliché, but the magnitude of the opportunities this new design presents to us is inspiring. We truly are in the sunrise phase, an organizational metamorphosis.

The transformation requires us to think in terms of architecture and space design as we create new environments, which are designed to keep people informed and help them communicate through increased involvement. The nine-point formula for success is an outline for the activities that a transformational environment should stimulate and encourage.

Education, learning and intellectual growth are at the heart of this transformation. The plethora of technological innovations are making us all students again.

Dr. Jim Crupi, a friend who teaches with Mike at AT&T's Center for Executive Education, run by the capable Deb Stout, says, "Education is the answer to our complex problems. But education is not merely for knowledge or more information. It is to make a difference in the world. It's about doing something and fixing what is wrong with our culture."

Jim is right on target. Those of us here have a rare opportunity to make a big difference in our world, and we can help achieve this through the way we design and create new spaces. Frank Lloyd Wright often said, "Architecture is the handmaiden of philosophy." We should ask, is our philosophy reflected in the way we use space? Is there a lag between what we envision for our home and work life and our personal and professional environments? Such a lag could be what's holding us back. Correcting that disparity in a meaningful and productive manner will require us to think out of the box together.

The Team Center™

The Team Center is one new architectural form meeting the needs of organizations intent on reengineering, creating boundaryless cultures, seamless structures, team-based leadership, virtual teams and drop-in or rendezvous environments. Whatever you're attempting to implement, attention to space and environmental issues is essential. The design and creation of appropriate environments for change and innovation are the physical manifestations of our commitment to psychological and philosophical innovation and growth.

Team Centers are fast becoming hubs in companies where people gather to work in contemporary modes and access the latest technological support. They are where people gather to get involved and become informed. The Creative Thinking Association of America pioneered the development of creative environments. At the time, there were few designers trumpeting the need for environmental evolution of spaces. Creative activities were often thought to be the sole dominion of R & D departments. The fight to get the business world to recognize the vital importance, not to mention the phenomenal financial rewards, of creativity has been an uphill struggle, but its importance is finally being recognized worldwide.

Team Centers are large group rooms in which people work, create and socialize together in a resource-rich environment with unique communications and creative thinking techniques. The Team Center is one of the most important physical spaces in any business or home, especially at a time when we're moving toward full implementation of team-based organizations and participatory workplaces. The Team Center is to a business or organization what a locker room is to athletics—a place to meet, plan strategy, create new plays, check equipment, assess the game, eat a snack, rebuild team spirit, bind wounds, etc. Locker room activities are essential to winning games, and what takes place in Team Centers is essential to achieving success in business and organizational life. To think out of the box, we need to be informed and involved—two of the many vital activities taking place in Team Centers.

The Team Center is also a gathering place for people working from home or telecommuting. People are social creatures. It's our nature to associate and relate to each other. In spite of telecommuting and the home office movement, very few people want to live as hermits. Experts believe there will come a time when most people will work exclusively from home. Nevertheless, among those who currently work from home, most want to drop in on occasion to touch base or socialize with other people involved in their work. The Team Center serves as a rendezvous environment for these people.

Jack Welch, GE's chairman, once described the Team Center this way: *One team. One room. One coffee pot. One vision.* Our company designed and built one of the first examples of GE's new group room concept at their locomotive division in Erie, Pennsylvania.

The interior design of Team Centers should weld current technologies with ample wall space reserved for high visualization techniques such as Displayed Thinking, process mapping, pert diagramming and other multi-functional organizational features. Their interior appointments should go far beyond the older, more simplistic technique called storyboarding.

The storyboard method was developed at The Walt Disney Company for use in motion picture planning. It later became the foundation for the Creative Thinking Technique System with the MICORBS™2 seven-step format. Storyboarding, as far as it goes, is merely a physical form employed for visualizing materials. People are often disappointed with the storyboard method because it doesn't include an action plan or what to do with the content or how to carry through to implementation.

The MICORBS seven-step format, which we explain further in Chapter 6, stands for:

Master Plan
Idea Development
Communications
Organization
Retrieval
Briefing Board
Synapse

It was invented to integrate classic organizational functions and the tools of the Creative Thinking Technique System into one system that is compatible with current electronic technologies and offers new leadership functions. We've learned through extensive experience with hundreds of companies that the MICORBS seven-step format should be included in the physical design to ensure measurable success.

2MICORBS™ is a registereed trademark of Intellectual Equities, Inc.

Thinking out of the box is a universal concept that serves a wide variety of organizations with diverse purposes and needs. Our company partners with leading architects, like Ziegler-Cooper of Houston, to develop creative environments unique to each organization and its needs. Some organizations to implement the Team Center concept include:

National Association of HomeCare
Entergy Utilities Company
General Electric
Glaxo Wellcome
Motorola
Norris Foods
Owens-Corning Fiberglas
CertainTeed
Rent-A-Center
Texas Eastern Products Pipeline Company
Methodist Hospital

These organizations represent a broad cross section of industries and markets, all of which benefit from thinking out of the box. Diverse organizations with diverse requirements especially need to engage in creative thinking practices to build inspiration, involvement and an exchange of critical information.

Five steps

There are five important steps to developing Team Centers in your organization.

Step 1. Train and familiarize the key players on the Team Center concept. Instruct them on the use of the Creative Thinking Technique System, featuring the MICORBS seven-step format, which is designed into the facility.

Step 2. Conduct a preliminary work session on the total project, including the master plan for the Team Center and methods for integrating the Creative Thinking Technique System into the culture of these organization. (Projects often go beyond the Team Center into a total building design or a redesign of an existing facility. The learning and designing process should be conducted in a participatory atmosphere.)

Step 3. Designers begin concept layouts, floor plans and drawings on the spot to be used for the Team Center.

Step 4. Concept design is completed and made into finished drawings to be given to a selected architect or contractor. (Our company usually stays involved through implementation to maintain continuity.)

Step 5. Design and complete a prototype project to demonstrate the capabilities and resources available through the new facility.

Our mission is to help revolutionize the way people work through the design of new transformational environments. Environment is certainly more than the physical space. An organization that wants to truly change the way its people think and work together must also transform its culture. The design of new cultures goes hand-in-hand with the design of new work environments. We spend considerable time cultivating company cultures. As the culture becomes enriched with new methods, the organization requires original and unique work spaces and habits.

Cultivating company cultures

The monumental transformation we spoke of at the beginning of this chapter makes it essential for organizations to reevaluate and, in many cases, develop an entirely new culture. The Creative Thinking Association of America specializes in diagnosing existing organizational cultures and works with teams to facilitate a plan to cultivate, transform and grow cultures into the next generation of that organization's business. Many people, because they are busy, think they can ignore their old culture and grow their business in spite of it. Unfortunately, that's like expecting the same old software to run differently on new hardware.

A unique example of cultivating a company culture took place at Apple Computer. We participated in a project during the startup phase of Apple in master planning the cultural goals of the new company. We refer to this project as the Apple Values Team. The values project was given considerable attention because it eventually led to the creation of one of the fastest growing, largest startup companies in the history of American entrepreneurship, with unprecedented dollar growth. Apple truly broke out of the box. In fact, it never got into the box to begin with.

One of the values we wanted to emphasize from the very start at Apple was open communications by design. Everybody was talking about open communications in those days, but it was a rare organization that really had them. Apple wanted people to speak out about their ideas and opinions. In other cultures, the unspoken rule has often been to clam up and not disclose ideas for fear of retribution or sanctions from the judge.

One of the models we used at Apple came from a story Mike had shared with A.C. (Mike) Markkula, cofounder and chairman, and Steve Jobs, also cofounder. The story told of a telephone call Mike received in his Disney office from the Yugoslavian government. While attending a conference at Harvard, someone had recommended to Marshal Tito that he should study the Disneyland University. The phone call was to arrange a visit from the number-two man in Yugoslavia, Secretary of the Economy Petrograd Savikovich. He arrived at Disneyland with full security and bulletproof limousines, with flags waving.

The secretary came into Mike's office and introduced himself. The textbook used in the Disney Way courses was on Mike's desk. The book, by Robert Shickle, was called *The Disney Version*, and it contained many negative critiques of the Disney company. Mike explained to the secretary that Disney believed in listening to what its adversaries had to say. The man didn't say a word in response. Mike then gave him the grand tour of Disneyland, and Savikovich was flabbergasted at the quality of the service, the employees' attitudes, the cleanliness and the many other factors that made the Disney experience so noteworthy. Throughout the day, if he asked Mike once, he asked him a thousand times (through a thick accent), "How do you get them to do what they do?" Mike admits that he was tempted to respond, "We have tanks hidden behind 'It's a Small World,' and, when people don't do what we tell them to do, we bring out the tanks and wipe out a bunch of them."

Back in the office, the secretary picked up *The Disney Version,* looked at Mike and said, "That's the difference between us. In my country, we would burn this book." That's what we're talking about when we refer to a different culture. How many organizations are you personally aware of where credos and mission statements grant lip service to a myriad of human-centered behaviors when, in reality, they roll out the tanks and wipe out a bunch of employees whenever people don't do what they're ordered to do? These are the cultures in need of transformation. Those who don't change will surely die out.

The Apple Values project adopted the philosophy of examining what adversaries say and using that information to instill and foster open communications within the culture. You don't have to worry about messengers with bad news being shot when the *enemy* is the bearer of bad news. But when a book critical to the current culture is burned, how likely is it that someone *within* the organization will step forward and say something similar—even if it needs to be said? Critical evaluation needs to be articulated to cleanse the organization of bad practices.

People do not live by process alone

Although we joke and poke fun at the various reengineering and reinventing projects going on in the corporate world today, we fully support most anything that makes a realistic analysis of the status quo and leads to improving conditions on any level. But just trying to bring about improvement isn't enough. All the good intentions in the world won't produce real solutions to complex problems. All the processes known to the human race, lined up end to end, won't result in a cultural transformation. If you glean no other message from this book, remember this one: A process alone does not make a cultural transformation. You and everyone in your organization must be part of the transformation because people are the transforming agents.

'Wizard of Oz Management'

The attitude, the caring and the cooperative spirit collectively have to be part of any change effort. It might sound soft, but it takes real courage to carry it off. Human-centered qualities should be part of your cultural transformation, or else you'll wind up further behind the eight-ball than you were before. We call this style of leadership "Wizard of Oz Management."

You have to get on a yellow brick road. The yellow brick road is your vision, your mission. It's the path on which you walk to get to the Emerald City where you will realize your vision. If there is no yellow brick road and no Emerald City, nothing will happen. You can't push people down the yellow brick road. You can't order them to march, like you could in Communist Yugoslavia. People have to be led down the yellow brick road. They have to want to get to the Emerald City so badly, they'll skip all the way.

There are three essential ingredients in the new cultures we help develop. Each ingredient is embodied in Wizard of Oz Management: brains, courage and heart. If you want to be part of the monumental transformation we described earlier, you must have all three. If you expect to lead your organization down the yellow brick road and realize your vision...if you want to make your mission statement come to life in the hearts of everyone you work with...if you expect to be part of the new dawn of technology and potential, two out of three won't do. Work toward your vision with all the passion you can muster. When you do, the others in the organization will contribute their brains, courage and hearts as well. Tell us what's soft about that.

Frank Lloyd Wright: Place

Mike was inspired by this great architect and had the chance to meet him in the late 1950s. Intrigued by his philosophies and works, Mike became an eager student of the man's work. He learned from his friend Kent Brandt, a retired architect from Columbus, Ohio, who was professor of architecture at Ohio State University. Mike attended lectures, followed the Mike Wallace interviews with Wright and yearned to become a fellow at the Frank Lloyd Wright Taliesin West Institute—a dream he never realized. He did, however, get to work with the Frank Lloyd Wright Home and Studio staff in Oak Park, Illinois, who are dedicated to keeping the Wright legacy alive. They invited him to help with their project because he had a unique grasp of Wright's philosophy. Mike was honored to help them develop ideas to further perpetuate the creative philosophy of Wright because his values, convictions and opinions are as provocative as his architecture.

The staff at Oak Park are genuinely concerned that some of Wright's ideas may be lost over time. They want to ensure that his ideas are not even watered down, much less forgotten. While too many of the buildings Frank Lloyd Wright (1869-1959) designed have been demolished, the staff guards against the destruction of his ideas.

When we forget the contributions of creative thinkers and innovators of the past, we hasten cultural disintegration. We're not saying only old ideas are worth honoring, but unique thinking has timeless value, whenever it occurs. Obviously, it's always a good practice to conserve constructive and worthwhile ideas. Let it not be forgotten that for one brief shining moment there was a Frank Lloyd Wright.

The Wright time

We worked with the Frank Lloyd Wright people using the Creative Thinking Technique and Displayed Thinking to create and capture plans and ideas for a Wright Time seminar. We devoted one Displayed Thinking board to an abbreviated biography of Wright for use in the seminar curriculum.

Wright studied under and worked with the notable architect Louis Sullivan, his mentor. During his illustrious career, Wright designed and built "prairie style" homes in and around Chicago. These homes were noted for their horizontal lines that hugged the landscape. Several examples have been carefully restored in the vicinity of his home and studio in Oak Park. You can visit these homes on a walking tour.

Wright was an iconoclast and a resolute minorist. He was a rebel whose causes were revolutionary structures and contemporary aesthetics. He also wedded machine methods and materials to create a matchless architectural expression. His innovations are legendary—open planning, elimination of traditional room divisions, fluid and flexible inner space, casement windows and spiral ramps. Some of Wright's major works include the Unity Temple in Chicago, the Hollyhock House in Los Angeles, the Imperial Hotel in Tokyo, the Taliesin West in Phoenix, Arizona, Falling Water in Pennsylvania and New York's Guggenheim Museum.

We had conversations with Elizabeth Wright-Ingraham, Wright's granddaughter and an architect from Colorado Springs. Elizabeth was on the team to maintain the rich heritage her grandfather left behind. In the time we spent with her, she never mentioned the weather, politics or other trivia. Her eyes twinkle with intelligence and a terrific sense of humor. Elizabeth autographed and presented us with a book about her grandfather titled *The Master Architect: Conversations with Frank Lloyd Wright*, edited by Patrick J. Meehan. We wish we could spend more time with people like Elizabeth.

> *"The ultimate creative thinking technique is to think like God.*
> *If you're an atheist, pretend how God would do it."*
>
> —Frank Lloyd Wright

Our conversations with Elizabeth and our extensive research of Wright's work gave us additional insights into this creative principle as well as Wright's total way of thinking about life and architecture. Elizabeth told us, "Grandfather spelled Nature with a capital 'N.' " Wright said many times, "To be truly creative, you have to be in league with Nature. Don't copy Nature, but see inside and come out with something new." We've highlighted some of Frank Lloyd Wright's other pronouncements:

"I believe in honest arrogance rather than hypocritical humility."

"You don't build a house on a hill—the house should be of the hill."

*"There are very few inferior people in the world;
there are only inferior environments."*

*"There will never be anything creative coming out of the education
which the teenager will receive today in his drift toward conformity."*

Lunch at Domino's

We worked with Tom Monohan, founder of Domino's Pizza, to build a Team Center in his spectacular corporate headquarters in Michigan. We talked with Tom at length about Frank Lloyd Wright. Tom is a Wright buff and collector of Frank Lloyd Wright memorabilia. He has a 10-foot wooden statue of Wright in his office. Wright has been an influence on Tom's thinking in a variety of ways. Someone who designs space the way Frank Lloyd Wright did looks at life differently than the average person. Wright was an out-of-the-box thinker in the truest sense of the term.

Artifacts

Two of the most profound creative principles Wright invoked were to think like God and impose no limitations. Wright's best practices include:

- Organic architecture.
- Prairie styling.
- Individualism.
- Vision.
- Open planning.

CHAPTER 5

Designing creative environments/ the enriched place

Don't let your environment control you. If it's not right, change it. Either we're in charge of our environment or it's in charge of us. Granted, there are always aspects of life that are beyond our ability to control, but there are few reasons to allow ourselves to be unnecessarily crippled and confined by an uncreative and demotivating atmosphere. Most of the time, we have the option of transforming our environments. If you're in a position of leadership, providing a creative, resource-rich environment for your organization is an opportunity you don't want to miss.

Clients and members of our seminar audiences often ask how we got interested in creative thinking and the challenge of cultural or environmental transformation. Business schools don't teach such subjects in significant depth and these questions are not on the agenda of enough business meetings. Because the creation of enriched environments is a more obscure topic of business discussion than, say, budget and bottom lines, people are naturally curious as to how we first became interested in the subject.

A short answer would be that Mike got interested in creative thinking from working in the Disney organization. It's true that the values Walt represented challenged Mike, along with everyone else who worked with him, to push his limits and to continue growing and developing as a person. Mike's life is vastly different today, as are the lives of millions, because of Walt Disney's influence.

But Mike's interest in environmental transformation started long before he became a part of the Disney team. In fact, at a luncheon Mike had with Walt and Los Angeles businessman Emmett McGaughey at the studio in the 1950s, they discussed Mike's thoughts about designing creative environments like the Kitchen for the Mind, something clearly dear to Walt's and Mike's hearts, of course. In fact, it was on this occasion of hearing Mike's Kitchen for the Mind concepts that Walt complimented him on the steps leading into the Disney's dining room, known as the Coral Room, saying, "Mike, you're one of the most creative guys I've met in a long time." Later, Walt's right-hand man, Card Walker, approached Mike about joining the Disney staff.

War-torn

Like most good things, Mike's focus on creating nurturing, healthy environments was borne out of conflict—while he was serving in the Korean War. This was the experience in Mike's life where conflict caused the pieces to start falling into place for him.

For Mike, the term "culture shock" first became real when he entered Seoul in 1952. Phrases like "war-torn country" are abstract to people who have never witnessed the devastation of war in person. Despite the news footage shot on the battlefield or superb descriptions from field correspondents, it's never real until you're actually there.

Seeing the bombed-out buildings of Seoul reminded Mike of skeletons, casting their eerie patterns on the moonlit landscape. Mike was soon to learn the vivid reality of war-torn people as well. Nothing stateside had adequately prepared him for the horrors of war. He was a warrant officer in the United States 7th Infantry Division, 31st Infantry Regent, otherwise known as the Polar Bears, stationed just above the

38th parallel—otherwise known as the front lines. Before Mike arrived, he was aware his assignment didn't offer favorable prospects of coming back unscathed or, for that matter, coming back at all. He saw many friends and comrades wounded or killed at Old Baldy Hill, the Jane Russell Hills and in the Tong Valley.

After Korea, Mike embraced Dr. Albert Schweitzer's doctrine of reverence for life, which became for him much more than a passage from a college philosophy textbook. Experiencing so much death made reverence for life a behavioral principle for Mike.

The war started for Mike when his troop ship docked at the Port of Inchon in December, 1952. The train ride to Seoul was arduous, setting the tone for the rest of his tour of duty. The troop train stopped frequently to clear the tracks of debris that rebels had placed there to block the trains on their journeys north. The debris on the tracks was a vivid reminder that there really was an enemy out there—a dangerous one. Each time the train stopped, hundreds of homeless children found the soldiers and beseeched them for food and handouts. The children were clothed in rags inadequate to protect them from the bitter cold.

Even though they clearly were children, the expressions on their faces and the look in their eyes made them appear 100 years old. Needless to say, these children made an impression on Mike—an impression that haunts him to this day. Indelibly etched in his mind is an image of forgotten children, abandoned like the discarded rubble piled by the rebels on the railroad tracks.

Merry Christmas

It was a snowy Christmas Eve before Mike finally arrived in Seoul. He was assigned a jeep and driver to transport him to his regiment. They left for the front immediately, driving through the snow flurries, which made it difficult to see in the dark. The road from Seoul to the MLR (Main Line of Resistance) was bumpy, pockmarked with pot holes. Suddenly, the jeep's headlights lit up a sign in front of them that read:

Light/helmet line. Lights out. Vests and helmets on. Now.

Mike swallowed hard. Both fear and excitement coursed through his veins. He knew the sign had a much deeper meaning than helmets and headlights. But there was no time to sit and contemplate. He and the driver were already wearing their helmets and flak jackets. The only things left to do were turn off the headlights and perhaps pray.

As they drove on through the darkness, keenly aware the enemy could now observe their movements, Mike thought to himself, *Merry Christmas*. The emotions stirred up by the ominous sign transported him back to earlier Christmases in Ohio. The flood of nostalgia left him feeling even lonelier on that sub-zero night on a remote road somewhere in Korea. The more alone and afraid he felt, the more Mike resolved to make it out of there and to get back home.

Facing the unfaceable

The jeep bumped along for a few more miles before it came upon an Army dump truck, which had pulled to the side of the road. The jeep driver pulled in behind the truck to check it out. The driver looked into the back of the uncovered transport and turned away, obviously disturbed. Mike walked toward the truck and asked him what he had seen. He said the sight was almost more than he could emotionally handle.

It was dark as Mike cautiously approached the truck. Seeing inside was difficult so he stepped up on the running board to peer into the truck bed. His entire body automatically convulsed, and a chill ran rapidly down his spine. Even in sub-zero temperatures, the chill was significantly cold. Inside the truck were the bodies of Korean children who had apparently frozen to death. Mike became nauseous. The sight brought him face to face for the first time with everyone's fragile mortality, including his own.

Six months after the truck incident, Mike was slightly injured on the line, enough to require a brief stay in a MASH hospital unit. The images of children begging beside the railroad tracks and the tiny corpses in the truck stayed with him. During his convalescence, he requested and was granted permission to help start and support an orphanage for displaced Korean children in Seoul. He and others secured an abandoned

Shinto temple that accommodated 50 children, which scarcely scratched the surface of the orphan problem. Soon, however, nearly every outfit in Korea was sponsoring an orphanage. (There are many of these Korean orphanages still operating today. Motorola asked Diane to work on a project in Seoul for one of their factories. Diane suggested that Mike visit one of these orphanages to see them again.)

This mission of mercy was supported through the philanthropy of the GIs and helped rebuild the spirit of both the children and the troops. Mike's appeal included a reminder to the GIs about how likely they were to get killed that night—a notion nobody argued with—and how meaningful a contribution to the orphanage would be. This typical situational GI humor caused many hardened soldiers to give everything they had, which wasn't much.

Exemplary acts are not reserved for the affluent alone. Those actually closest to the problem are usually the ones who give the most and work the hardest on a cause. These experiences helped Mike to understand why it's vital to involve people closest to the problem in designing and implementing solutions. Creativity will flourish when people's desire is aroused to do something about a need. People begin to think out of the box when their passions are aroused.

Thinking out of the bag

The following story was the one Walt Disney heard Mike tell at lunch before Mike was approached by Card Walker to join the Disney team. Mike began by describing how, between the enemy's violent outbursts, they waited and waited and waited. The political stalemate over the war that wasn't supposed to be a war began grinding them down. As soldiers, their lives bounced back and forth between boredom and sheer terror.

Enemy infiltrators, Chinese and North Korean soldiers who periodically punched through the lines, could come screaming through a soldier's trench or bunker at any time—usually at night. Mike suffered from the same constant fear that enveloped the soldiers and other officers. One night, Mike's regiment suffered an attack from the infiltrators. In spite of the fact the soldiers slept with a loaded side arm on their chests and an M-1 rifle next to them, the infiltrators were on Mike and his comrades too quickly. A number of soldiers around Mike died before they could wake up and defend themselves.

Even more frightening than the infiltrators, who sometimes operated a mile behind the lines, were the air bursts from American artillery shells. The artillery behind Mike's lines fired over his head and, occasionally, a shell would burst above the troops and rain shrapnel down upon them. A couple of soldiers in Mike's bunker died from friendly-fire wounds.

At the time, Mike inscribed his thoughts in a journal he maintained throughout the Korean war:

"We spend too much time in our sleeping bags trying to escape the bitter cold weather. You get a false sense of security huddled up in these bags. I've got to get out of this bag, even though it's freezing-cold outside. I've been in here most of the time for nearly two months without changing anything. The time has come for me to make over this stinking sleeping bag into an enriched environment.

"We've been reduced to moles living under the ground—I'm a frigging ground hog who has been to college. What a shitty way to exist. How did I get here anyway? How do I get out?

"There is no denying of reality; reality is, this is our life when we're not moving locations, fighting, eating, going to the outhouse or jumping into bunkers to dodge incoming mail [artillery and mortar shells].

"Our life is lived curled up in sleeping bags freezing our asses off when they stick out too far.[1] I have to get a life. I have to change this God-awful way of living.

"I'm going to declare Groundhog Day and cast a shadow. I've made a fundamental discovery inside my sleeping bag—I have discovered 'I.' 'I' had been the ninth letter of the alphabet, something I said to indicate 'me.' Now, 'I' was 'me.'

"Zipped up inside my sleeping bag on a cold night, I learned just how close I am to myself. It's like this also when you're in a hospital bed.

---

[1]There was a great deal of frostbite among the troops.

"I really hear myself breathing. I smell my own body odors. I taste myself inside my mouth. I am hands, feet and teeth."

While cocooned in his sleeping bag, Mike felt as if Abraham Maslow's spirit was in there with him. Human needs became more real to Mike than they ever had before. Living as comfortably as most people do in the United States, we often take needs for granted. Only when comforts have been almost completely denied do we begin to take them seriously. When Mike was in college, Maslow's hierarchy of human needs had been an interesting concept. Now, Mike's heightened sense of even the most basic human needs launched him into his awkward journey of discovery.

Experience is always the best teacher of principles. Nearly 40 years before such words became part of our parlance, Mike set out to create a virtual world inside his sleeping bag. The odds were high that, like so many around him, his sleeping bag was going to be his last residence on earth. He decided to take charge of his environment. It wasn't good enough anymore to simply huddle from the cold and hope an enemy soldier wouldn't catch him unawares.

The first act Mike did was to improvise some type of wall to define the virtual room within. He scavenged the discarded ends from 155mm Howitzer wooden ammo boxes and strapped them together in a "U" shape, two sides and a top, then positioned the little structure where it would span his waist. The shell box walls held up the top of the bag to form a small room. Next, he fashioned a door by placing a tent pole on either side of his head to hold up the sleeping bag flaps. He dubbed the new space he had created a "head room." He covered the walls with paper to create storyboards where he could draw the pictures in his mind.

With the flaps closed against the cold, he was in total darkness. Like many people, Mike could have chosen to simply stay in the dark. But he was on a roll. He was intent on creating an environment for the living. To provide light, he envisioned track lighting—but this was the battlefront in war-torn Korea. He had no budget to pay for the equipment, even if it had been available. Worse yet, he didn't have a brochure to tell him how to do it! (How did God create the heavens and the earth without a brochure? We've read the book of Genesis many times and nowhere does it say, "In the beginning, God created a brochure...") Mike created his track lighting with flashlights taped to the tent poles and it worked out nicely—"flashtrack lights."

With temperatures down to 10 degrees below zero, Mike contemplated how to warm up his virtual world. Soldiers were issued hand warmers, which were fueled by cigarette lighter fluid. Mike's hand warmer became the potbellied stove in his little living space. The hand warmer heated the space so well, Mike sometimes opened up the flaps to lower the temperature.

Mike was constantly hungry in his new head room. A can of "C" rations (cookies) positioned by his right shoulder came next. There was no question Mike was moving up Maslow's hierarchy of needs one notch at a time. As each basic human need was satisfied with innovation and ingenuity, Mike moved to the next. "C" rations tasted pretty bad in those days, so he filled a canteen with coffee and added a lot of sugar for dunking. As Mike defined it: "Dunking allows you to immerse something shitty in something not so shitty so you can stand to eat it."

The principle of dunking applies to both the literal and figurative swallowing of something undesirable. Admittedly, Mary Poppins couched the same concept more gently with her "spoonful-of-sugar helps-the-medicine-go-down" remedy. Realistically, we're called upon to dunk more often than we might think. Making do with what we have and dunking are two of the unnoticed but valuable creative principles we can learn.

With more and more of Mike's basic needs fulfilled, he turned to aesthetic accoutrements. He acquired a radio and positioned it at his left shoulder. Mike tuned in to classical concerts in his virtual room. One of his favorites, broadcast on the Far East Command radio station, was Tchaikovsky's *1812 Overture*. On one occasion, Mike and his troop amplified the *1812 Overture* on loudspeakers aimed in the direction of "no man's land." (They had their own cannons for special effects!) It scared the enemy to death. It was a brief diversion amid the chaos and boredom. It gave the men a much-needed moment to think out of their collective box.

There were no cellular phones in the 1950s, but Mike had the ever-reliable "walkie-talkie" for communications in the field. He kept a walkie-talkie on his left side, which kept him in contact with the outside world. Mike often talked with guys from their artillery positions, inviting them over to share a cup of coffee at his sleeping bag. Mike's sleeping bag became a gathering place for fellowship and the swapping of war stories and tales of women they had known. Social activities need gathering places, whether they be in the physical or the "wired" world. Gathering places and the social activities that take place there stimulate out-of-the-box thinking.

Security becomes a prime concern when you're buttoned up in a bag, especially with the considerable infiltration activity from enemy patrols at night. Mike placed trip wires and connected cans filled with rocks at intervals around the perimeter. Intruders trying to sneak through the wire would sometimes rattle the cans, alerting "residents." This was Mike's version of a security system, without the monthly charges.

Despite the crude but effective security system, the enemy still managed to surprise the soldiers from time to time and some lost their lives in their sleeping bags. For further protection, Mike managed to lay his hands on a B.C. scope, a heat-sensing camera, that worked on an infrared principle. He made a small opening at the top of the enclosure for the scope. Thanks to the night vision technology, Mike could see through the dark and detect any suspicious movement. Whenever you're buttoned up in a bag, it helps to have a scope to let you see through the dark.

A Kitchen for the Mind

There were a variety of other items in Mike's bag to aid in his survival and sanity—family pictures, books, writing paper, crayons and, of course, himself. He decided to call this virtual room a Kitchen for the Mind. We have kitchens to satisfy the needs of the stomach, but no comparable room dedicated to the needs of one of our most important organs—the brain. After duty, Mike couldn't wait to get back to his kitchen for a cup of hot coffee, some dunked 'C' rations, some good music, a book, to write a letter or look at pictures of loved ones, talk on the walkie-talkie, sketch on his storyboards and scope the landscape after dark.

When you stop and think about the incredible technology Mike had in his sleeping bag on a remote Korean battlefield over 40 years ago, the most fascinating fact was that no one was using it in the creative way Mike used it. To his surprise, others began to create similar environments for themselves. They didn't copy Mike's exactly but added their own creative touches. They called the Kitchen for the Mind a hootch, a term used again in Vietnam.

Through Mike's sleeping bag experience, he learned important lessons about leadership and stimulating creativity. One of the most important leadership techniques he learned is to prototype and lead by example, demonstrating for everyone that you believe in what you're asking them to do. Actions are always more convincing than words. Leaders must be willing to practice what they preach. One of our mottos is: Don't talk about it—prototype it. Go light on the preaching and heavy on the prototyping. If you really want to get people moving in a certain direction, don't numb their brains with a lot of talk. Just prototype the idea and keep quiet. Leaders, teachers and parents need to be living examples of what they believe in and the values they want to promote.

The power of a good idea

The Kitchen for the Mind concept, the hootch, caught on among the men around Mike and spread to other units across the entire front like wildfire—without orders being issued to immediately convert sleeping bags into Kitchens for the Mind. The men did it because there was a need, and it only takes one person to start the solution train rolling. Good ideas are sometimes embraced quickly if people recognize their value. As Thomas Edison said, "I want to invent things that people really want."

The improvised habitat groundswell Mike started in Korea proved that each one of us is creative when we are stimulated—when we remember that, as Buckminster Fuller said, we live in a creative universe. What we need is a catalyst, or yeast, if you will, to help us rise to the challenge. Often the virtual rooms other GIs put together were spectacular examples of ingenuity. They weren't college graduates or architects. What they needed was a model to spark their own creativity and imagination. Mike was one of the lucky ones. Creativity was encouraged when he was growing up. Creating his first Kitchen for the Mind in Korea was a natural outgrowth of the type of creativity that had been encouraged in him for a long time.

It's important to know it's never too late to develop habits that let creativity flow through us. People are inventive, ingenious, innovative and industrious if they are only motivated occasionally. As written in his journal at the time, Mike and his fellow infantrymen had been living in their bags like moles even as the resources to change their quality of life were everywhere around them. It's revealing to note Mike didn't attempt to do anyone's thinking for them. Creativity is stimulated by leaders who set the example and demonstrate the results. People will do their own thinking soon enough if you let them.

Without question, Mike's Korean experience launched his enthusiasm for creating enriched environments and the multitudes of benefits that come with them. The Team Center concept in business provides a social gathering place, filled with tools, resources, people, food, music and unique learning materials to stimulate creative thinking. Frank Lloyd Wright called such places "resource-rich environments," a concept echoed and applied by Dr. Maria Montessori in her classrooms.

Just as Mike's improved sleeping bag in Korea helped him to maintain his sanity and have a more enriched life amid the travail, good morale in your organization is essential to help your people survive through tough times and thrive in spite of them. Virtual rooms on the battlefront had a marked impact on the morale of the troops as times got even tougher.

Tuning up for battle

The overture to battle has a distinct sound to those who have experienced combat. Mike and fellow infantrymen heard the distant rumble of the Chinese tanks as they moved into position. Then they heard the rumble of their own armor moving up to counter the attack. American artillery began pounding enemy positions on Old Baldy relentlessly at about midnight. Tanks and infantry were moving into position in front of no man's land, illuminated by the eerie glow of flares, shot off by both sides high into the air. The rumbling and clanking sounds of battle echoed through the Tong Valley as if it were a huge orchestra tuning up for a concert. The Army Corps of Engineers fired up their smoke generators after dawn and laid down a curtain of artificial smoke through the valley to cover troop movements like clouds hiding in the moon.

Mike could see North Korean soldiers coming over the hill only several hundred yards away, with their bayonets fixed and their "potato masher" grenades swinging from their belts. Everyone knew this was clearly real. Not virtual reality—but life-and-death reality. The battle raged for several days and nights, with each side pushing the other back and then regaining ground. The enemy punched through American lines numerous times, causing Mike and other soldiers to watch their rears as well as the forces attacking from the front.

When the battle for Old Baldy was over, the mountain was nearly 20 feet shorter. The top of the mountain had literally been blown away by the unceasing artillery barrage. In the end, neither side had gained anything. Nevertheless, the Combat Infantryman's Badge that Mike was awarded following that battle is one of his most prized possessions to this day.

Fighting for your life is an act of passion in its most primitive state. Many of us experience varying levels of passion depending on the activity in which we're engaged. Whether we're fighting for our lives or fighting for market share, trying to save a failing company or a failing marriage, striving for recognition in our field or reaching out to a troubled young person, the degree of our passion will play a major role in determining our success.

The Kitchen comes home

The Kitchen for the Mind had its origin in Mike's grubby sleeping bag on the front line in Korea. He returned from Korea to finish his undergraduate work at Ohio State University in Columbus, Ohio. Mike and his wife lived in a one-room apartment with a pullout bed, a pullout kitchen with a pullout stove and pullout children! It was immediately clear that they needed to apply the lessons Mike learned in transforming his sleeping bag environment in Korea. Mike took his family's living space and transformed it into a Kitchen for the Mind. At the time, Mike called it a place to make banana cakes for the head.

Several years later, after they moved into a house, he noticed that most people's living rooms looked remarkably alike; a three-cushion sofa, an end table with a lamp, a coffee table and a dying African violet. People used their living rooms as a place to vacuum and dust. Then there was usually another room called a den, a family room, a library, the great room or, if you go back far enough, a rumpus room. It was a cheap version of the living room, with the decor of an economy motor lodge and vinyl furniture that stuck to any exposed part of your body whenever you got up to walk away.

Mike transformed the living room in his first house into a Kitchen for the Mind. Since then, every home he's lived in has had a Kitchen for the Mind. Every version seems to get more imaginative, including the latest version in Mike's Florida home. Designing your Kitchen for the Mind is half the fun of it. We highly recommend you take a space in your home and make it a place that stimulates you to think out of the box. If you'd like, you can send a picture of your Kitchen for the Mind to our address listed in the back of this book.

If you're in a leadership position, it's important that you encourage everyone in your organization to create a Kitchen for the Mind in their homes. We don't leave our brains at the office or factory when we go home because they are, hopefully, attached to us. Some of the most productive ideas and breakthroughs come late at night or on weekends or while doing a totally unrelated activity. Make a conscious effort to surround yourself with the tools and resources for thinking out of the box. If you work from home, you need a creative environment to make it exciting and stimulating.

Furnishing your kitchen

Think of the kitchen for your stomach. You have the necessary utilities to transform recipes into wonderful food for eating. In the Kitchen for the Mind, you have magnificent utilities to create wonderful resources to feed your spirit and intellect. In your kitchen for the stomach, you have breakfast, lunch, dinner and snacks. In your Kitchen for the Mind, you work on projects, programs, celebrations and individual activities, cooking up recipes as you go.

Technology helped set the stage for the Kitchen for the Mind as people began to cluster around the television. Later, the VCR gave us more control over television viewing. If you have several children, having several VCRs will help to avoid letting television get control over them. Video games and home computers belong here, too. The walls of your Kitchen for the Mind should have lots of space to pin up concepts and ideas. Track lighting illuminates the walls and highlights your Displayed Thinking. Mike has a microscope for inspecting the small picture and a telescope for surveying the big picture, as well as a planetarium that projects the night sky on the ceiling. And don't forget musical instruments, board games, a stereo and anything else that gets your creative juices flowing.

As mentioned earlier, Disney vice president Card Walker approached Mike and explained that Disney had a type of Kitchen for the Mind at the studio. They called it a team unit, around which offices were clustered. They already had the spirit for what we call the Kitchen for the Mind and had given it a business application.

After Mike began working for Disney, he began calling the individual units a Team Center. We've made a semi-career out of designing Team Centers, products for Team Centers and techniques for working in team environments for clients around the world. As cultures become more collaborative, the demand for environments and methodologies that support team efforts is increasing. Our experience indicates that the new management and leadership concepts—such as reengineering, boundaryless TQM, empowerment programs, open-book leadership—succeed best when placed in a Team Center environment. Team Centers, or group rooms as they're sometimes referred to, operate on much of the same principles as the Kitchen for the Mind in the home.

Tasks in enriched places

The four activities that take place in the Kitchen for the Mind are the same tasks that take place in any creative environment—projects, programs, celebrations and individual or personal activities.

Projects. Projects are activities you're creating at home—such as family vacations—or at work—such as redesigning the General Electric locomotive.

Programs. A program is sharing and communicating what you've created. Displayed Thinking is especially valuable in not only helping to visualize the creative process, but also to communicate the results through programs.

A program we conducted at Walt Disney World was a huge party to help everyone working on the site to understand what the park was going to be like and how it was going to work. The program helped them understand the project.

A program related to the family vacation project might be a video production of your experiences.

Celebrations. Celebrations are times to socially recognize accomplishments and efforts. They are awards programs. The more people work in teams, the more recognition is necessary. Celebrations also help connect individuals who are interconnected through technology as new work forms evolve.

Personal activities. Everyone has interests near and dear to their hearts. Enriched environments exist to involve, inform and inspire not just teams, but individuals as well. Teams are associations of several individuals, and it's important to pique everyone's interest and give creative juices somewhere to flow.

Whether they be musical, mathematical, microprocessor or mental telepathy, the interests of the individual must have a central place in the creative environment.

Projects, programs, celebrations and individual activities ideally take place regularly in enriched environments. If the Team Center is a dull place, it's not a real Team Center. The proof of how successful your creative environment is can be measured by what goes on there and how much it is in demand by users.

Displaying your thinking brings ideas to life in a special way and engages the whole group in the creative thinking process. Mike's office at the Disney Studios was adjacent to his unit's Team Center on the fourth floor of the Animation Building. In the Team Center was a wall approximately 30 feet long, covered by drapes that could be drawn back. Mounted on the wall behind the drapes were the unit's storyboards. The secret wall was actually created by accident.

Mike and his group were studying the philosophy and traditions of the company, in order to develop a training and development program and anticipate the tremendous personnel needs created by the future opening of Walt Disney World in Orlando.[2] Mike and others pinned cards to the wall with various ideas and tenets they thought contributed to the culture Walt had created. Soon, they were simultaneously becoming increasingly involved and informed as each one communicated with the other.

The information on the wall grew and grew. The team individually put up all their ideas, including Walt. Other ideas would mysteriously appear, authored by unidentified sources, or pinned up by someone late at night or from another unit. During this period, Mike's knowledge of leadership grew and developed into the beginnings of his personal philosophy for leadership.

'Bumble bee management'

The story is told about Hayley Mills, a British teen actress shooting a film at the Disney studio. She asked Walt what he did around the

---

[2]Mike was meeting with Card Walker and Don Tatum, trying to decide what to call the companywide management development campaign. Several ideas were bounced around until finally Card suggested they call the process organizational development (OD). Mike used the new term in a speech at the ASTD convention in Anaheim, and a new function of human resources was born.

company. She asked if he ran a camera. He replied that he didn't. She asked if he drew animated figures. He told her he once did, but had since hired much more talented artists to do that. As the conversation went on, the actress was increasingly curious about whether Walt actually did any work.

Walt finally said to her, "I'm like a bumble bee. I go from project to project carrying pollen." Hayley still didn't completely understand. But Mike and his colleagues did. Mike calls this "bumble bee management." In Walt's floor plan at the studio, they had designed creative pods where teams would work on specific projects. Walt constantly wandered down the main hallway and dropped in to check on the progress of each team. He didn't do their thinking for them, but he constantly challenged their thinking, which made them work even harder and clearly stimulated their creativity. At the end of a day, Walt often invited the team members from the various team units to come have a drink with him at the Coral Room on the lot. He truly believed in dialogue and interchange. As a bumble bee, he mixed creative pollen from many sources. (He also had a sting that he used when needed.)

Units become Team Centers

The Disney organizational development (OD) program was head-quartered in the animation building,[3] in Unit 3-D, near Walt's office at the studio in Burbank. The actual contents of Walt's office were moved from Burbank and are on display in the waiting area for the "Great Moments with Mr. Lincoln" attraction at Disneyland. The office display looks exactly as it did when Walt was alive, including the views from his windows. Walt occasionally stuck his head into the OD area to kibitz on his way to or from his office. Mike was on the bottom of the management

---

[3]The animation building, built on the eve of the World War II, was designed to look like a hospital from the outside. Fears of Japanese bombing on the West Coast led to other strange decisions in and around Hollywood. Lockheed had a plant next to the Burbank airport, a likely military target in the event of a Japanese raid. Warner Brothers didn't want their sound stages to be mistaken for a defense plant by Japanese pilots. So they painted the word "Lockheed" on the roof of one enormous sound stage with an arrow pointing toward the Burbank airport.

chart, but his proximity to Walt and Walt's interest in people development gave him spontaneous and informal contact unknown to others in the organization. Mike's OD participants were lucky to have the opportunity for similar spontaneity—quick and to-the-point hallway conversations with the torchbearer of the company.

The OD center housed the teams' work area, Mike's office and a space for Mike's associate, Pam Cannell. They were also adjacent to the main story conference room, which was a hub of activity at the studio. Their facility was filled with resources, archival materials and storyboards. Conceptually, Mike's office was a small Team Center. He had a wall approximately 30 feet long with curtains that could be opened and closed to cover the storyboards behind them. The wall became a sort of blueprint for the Disney Way, as it displayed the essence of the concepts and philosophies Mike and his associates were learning.

Replicating success

At the time, it occurred to Mike that they were uncovering some of the best-kept creative secrets of highly creative people who had extraordinary creative track records. Their credentials were unquestionable and universally respected. They were the creators of *Snow White and the Seven Dwarfs, Fantasia, The Living Desert Series, Mary Poppins,* Disneyland and an endless list that garnered 41 Academy Awards and 36 Emmys to that time.

The really big, albeit virtually untold, story was how the Disney teams accomplished such phenomenal success. What were their secrets? How did they think? How did they actually work? What made them tick? At the time the concept of organizational development was launched, Bob Matheison, a Disney executive, and Mike had to face the challenge of helping to groom leadership that would keep the creative process alive. There were new chapters to be written in the saga.

Card Walker understood the concept of teaming individuals together in a sort of buddy system. That's how Bob and Mike ended up working together. Card had been impressed with the fact that Mike had written and produced a TV show called "Men At the Top" and had managed to get it on the air without any inside political connections. Being a young guy from Ohio who grew up in a home where his mother was a get-things-done kind of person,[4] Mike didn't realize it was impossible to launch a television show by himself. Card remarked to Don Tatum that they should hire Mike. To Card, also a get-it-done kind of guy, Mike's TV achievement was a major credential.

Even so, because Mike was a person who had not been "raised" within the Disney system, he was teamed with Bob Matheison, who was a Disney veteran. Without Bob's assistance and insight, Mike couldn't have been nearly as effective in his job. Bob operated with a great deal of common sense and had an unflinching loyalty to Walt and the principles he stood for. Card once said to Mike, "Bob is just an all 'round good guy. We need more like him. He is a Disney guy." He was right. Any organization should strive to have well-rounded people like Bob Matheison.

When you're attempting to deal with the entire philosophy of a company, you'll naturally encounter some petty politics along the way. There are people in any organization who, intentionally or unintentionally, block the organization from taking an honest and fearless self-inventory. Bob Matheison is the opposite of such people. He represents the dedicated hard workers who don't get sucked into pointless politics. He's always aware of the more important purpose at hand. The best trained and educated person in the world who is stuck in the quagmire of petty politics isn't worth a fraction of what an enthusiastic, dedicated hard worker is worth.

People who are truly dedicated to the philosophy and boast a track record to match help others to rise above the mundane to a higher plateau. Mike was in his early 30s when he joined the Disney organization and made his share of youthful mistakes. Instead of coming down on Mike, Bob encouraged him. He helped Mike learn the value of second

---

[4]Mike's mother, Virginia Vance, was a National Girl Scout commissioner in the Midwest. She frequently took award-winning girls to Washington, D.C., for recognition of their accomplishments. In 1947, a Black girl among her small group was refused a room at the Washington hotel where they had reservations. Virginia had the whole group sit down in the lobby until the girl was admitted with the rest. Virginia Vance was an early activist.

chances. Creativity flourishes in environments where people are encouraged to take risks.

Best-kept secrets

Realizing how valuable the information was on the 30-foot wall in Mike's office, his team named the wall "best-kept secrets." The information was not literally meant to be kept a secret to avoid industrial espionage. Secrets remain secrets, in the deepest sense, until someone understands them enough to take action. An informal ritual grew around this wall and the manner in which the cards were shown to members of the OD programs and curious visitors who were interested in the insights they contained.

This ritual was a fun way to share philosophical and conceptual knowledge, and it heightened people's curiosity about what new information was displayed there. No one ever made a big deal out of this ritual. Mike and his unit didn't even talk about it much. But the idea of thoughts being displayed was intriguing nonetheless.

Louis Lundborg, then Bank of America chairman, said of the wall, "What a tremendous idea. It's intriguing. Whoever thought of hiding your philosophy behind a curtain? I love it. I'm going to do it." Fred D. Learey, then chairman of General Telephone of Florida, also commented on the wall, "Mike, you've got some of the best-kept secrets of highly creative people here."

The wall forced Mike and others to pin down creativity and put it on display. It also forced them to capture the essence of creative principles and express them in simple terms so they could get a handle on the process. The wall helped keep them realistic. The experience of creating in such an atmosphere is hard to describe in words. Language is too limiting. Yet, the intuitive nature of creating is known to anyone who has enjoyed the experience. Give your important ideas and principles a special place to reinforce their value.

Even though the OD unit was filled with hundreds of books on innovation, imagination and originality that Mike and his team diligently studied, none of the volumes adequately captured the illusive commodity that came to be known as the Disney Way. Books on creativity continue to be extremely complex and protracted. They mostly describe the creative achievements of people rather than explaining how to stimulate creative thinking.

Admittedly, the how-to of creativity is difficult to isolate. And far be it from us to oversimplify the profound human experience of creativity. However, the fundamental principles of creative thinking are known to most everyone. It's not a matter of whether a person possesses creative energies and resources — it's a matter of whether he or she is motivated to use them. A leader who accuses his or her people of being uncreative is usually self-indicting. The truth is, this leader probably hasn't created the motivational atmosphere to launch his or her people into action.

In spite of all this, Mike and other Disney unit members had to take a stab at naming the creative process on the secret wall. They had to somehow package the Disney Way and transmit it into the future. They needed to fully understand and be able to teach the best-kept secrets and best practices, which some writers have called Disney Magic. They had to fashion creative tools to help continue the creative craft.

Tools

The nine-point formula for success (explained in Chapter 3) is built on the principles behind the drapes. The best-kept secrets of some of the world's most creative people are at your fingertips when you combine $I^3 + P^3 > C^3$ with vision and methods. The storyboard method from the Disney studios has evolved into the Displayed Thinking system we now teach through the Creative Thinking Association of America. Displayed Thinking immediately involves people. Participation is unavoidable. The legend of the wall continues, as Displayed Thinking gets people involved, keeps them informed and inspires them to think out of the box!

As you begin the transformation process in your organization, you will find, as we did, that involved, informed and inspired people begin to change not only the way leadership leads, but how the entire company operates. It wasn't our initial intent to describe an operational philosophy for the entire company, but that's what happened. The Disney

Way was not a program exclusively for developing management. Every Disney employee was educated in the Disney Way. What we ended up developing was a way for every Disney employee to be involved and informed and to communicate with each other and with customers who, at Disney, are referred to as guests.

Laurels are not for resting on

Disney was already an international household word by the time Mike set to work on the Disney Way. With a famous name and reputation for exceptional creativity, customer service and customer relationships, the Florida operation, which was scheduled to open in 1971, would have to hit the bricks running. The moment the doors were opened, the public would expect everything to meet Disney standards. Card Walker said, "We have to start off at Walt Disney World with the quality we have [evolved] at Disneyland, from day one. We'll be judged right from the beginning. There won't be a honeymoon period for us."

Card was challenging us to think out of the box before there was a box! The creative process had to be applied in advance. Like Walt Disney World, you and your organization are probably judged by standards already established for your industry. You don't have time to mess around in the marketplace, either. It's always best to establish standards and values early on because of the impact they'll have on your creativity.

Unlike much of what's passed off as organizational development today, OD at Disney originally stood for any activity that helped the organization grow and improve. The first Disney OD program had six main objectives:

1. To educate Disney people about every aspect of the company, top to bottom.
2. To give everyone the opportunity to study and visit every nook and cranny throughout the entire organization.
3. To give everyone the opportunity to meet and talk with nearly every department head about their area and leadership style.

4. To bring people together with top executives for an evening meal, often lasting between six and eight hours, to discuss company philosophy, values, standards, history, policy, Walt and the Disney Way.

5. To bring people together for "best practices luncheons" with outstanding senior executives from other companies and expert speakers to conduct leadership symposiums with the OD members on an exchange basis.

6. To complete special research projects on company problems. The best practices of benchmarking foster high standards for creativity. Actual projects, rather than case studies, strengthen the creative muscle.

Our first OD group lasted six months.[5] It consisted of seven people who were being groomed for higher positions. Their special research project was studying the entrance complex for Walt Disney World. Formally presenting their findings to Walt himself was the highlight of this inaugural group's experience. There was a lot of give-and-take at the session. Afterward, the whole group joined Walt in the Coral Room for drinks, dinner and further discussion. (This OD briefing occurred shortly before Walt entered Saint Joseph's Hospital for tests that would bring grim news.)

Mike vividly recalls that stimulating experience with Walt and Card. No one seemed more enriched and inspired by the event than Walt himself. He had a great time with that group. The way Walt shared his visionary thinking for the future inspired countless creative ideas and challenges within the group. It's a shame these OD practices were developed at the end of Walt's life and not much earlier. Yet, he set in motion creative initiatives and leadership practices that are as valid today as they were during his lifetime. Models of creative thinkers are more valuable than theories about creative thinking.

---

[5]The only real chewing-out Mike ever received from Walt or Roy Disney occurred unexpectedly in the hallway when Mike neglected to invite the spouses of the OD group to a retreat they held in La Jolla. Walt and Roy were great believers in having a strong and supportive family unit who understood the company's philosophies. They included the spouses thereafter. Spouses were also invited to the studio for a briefing on the Disney Way and the Florida project and lunch in the Coral Room.

A long-term investment

These highly participatory programs continued for seven years, and prepared the cadre for Walt Disney World and other Disney ventures. Dick Nunis, chairman of Walt Disney Attractions, gave considerable time and contributed extensively to the understanding of Walt and the concept of organizational creativity. What Dick has forgotten about the theme park business is by itself more than anyone will ever know to begin with.

Dick and Mike have very different personality types and didn't see eye to eye on many issues, but that never got in the way of what they were trying to accomplish because the stage was so well set under Walt's and Card's leadership. Dick and Mike spent many hours together at OD dinners, conferences and sitting in bars, talking about their favorite subject—Walt. (After conversing one night until 3:00 a.m., they both overslept and showed up late for a meeting with then chairman Don Tatum. To make matters worse, Mike was supposed to be in charge of the meeting. Dick got a bang out of his predicament. Don wasn't the least bit amused.)

Disney policymakers invested time, money and other resources to inform and communicate—to involve and educate—future leaders at Disney. No stone was left unturned in nurturing the company's greatest asset: its evolving leadership.

Information is information

Not only did Disney people read the books written by Disney adversaries, they debated them openly. The content of their OD sessions was never one-sided pro-Disney propaganda. Walt and Roy were especially interested in what competition and critics had to say about their operation. They believed that burying their heads in the sand would have been suicidal. Unlike the archetypal executives, Walt and Roy wanted to hear the bad news along with the good news, even when they didn't like it. They didn't shoot the messengers just because they brought bad news. In fact, Walt solicited honest feedback from people at all levels of the organization,[6] even though the process got testy at times, to say the least.

A story, perhaps a bit apocryphal, is often told in Disney OD programs about how, when Walt suspected something was missing from any attraction or movie, he didn't huddle exclusively with his directors and designers to figure out what was wrong. He would gather people at a table, perhaps in a restaurant, and ask a waitress or a busboy to join them. Walt believed creativity also came through people who have different points of departure. He used to say that some of the best ideas come from kids and their mothers.

From Disney story conference to charrette

In Walt's day, a Disney story conference was an open exchange, to say the least. We took this practice and developed it into what we now call a charrette. As an intensive schooling on a specific project, a charrette produces extremely valid conclusions. In fact, years of experience indicate six-month studies won't necessarily produce more reliable information than a charrette lasting only a few days. A typical charrette involves a team set up in a special unit, or Team Center, that works intensely using Displayed Thinking to develop a master plan and take a stab at a preliminary conclusion regarding the project or problem.

Most project teams fiddle around too much because the team has been given little, if any, structure and organization within which to operate. The concept of organization and free-flowing creativity might sound mutually exclusive, but they're not. The highest creativity occurs in well-organized environments. Poor organization leads to wasted time and confusion. Confused people are not creative people.

Conflict and creativity

A mark of quality leadership is facing criticism head on. Taking what people say about you seriously is not easy to do. You might have to

---

[6]When the Yugoslavian official had finished his tour of Disneyland, Mike gave him the book that was critical of Disney. Mike wanted to show how Disney actually acknowledged its opposition—rather than ordering arrests and interrogations at secret police headquarters.

face the fact that you're doing some tasks wrong. We recommend you seek out and study what your adversaries and critics say about you. At Disney, Mike and his peers constantly analyzed their strengths and weaknesses. They debated their philosophy. There were heated arguments over policy. And they read the books and articles Disney critics wrote.

The cord binding them together through many of their disagreements at Disney was their allegiance to the underlying principles, values and objectives they subscribed to. No amount of criticism from the outside could fracture a bond forged with principles and values. A genuine, resource-rich, creative environment that is protected and nurtured follows Walt Disney's admonition to add value to whatever you do. Involved, informed and inspired people, working in a resource-rich place, developing new and improving existing products and services, produce caring, cooperative and creative leadership.

Dr. J. Vernon Luck: People

Mike first met Dr. Luck in 1959 at the First Congregational Church in Los Angeles. The doctor and his wife, Ramona, befriended Mike when he was new to the area. Dr. Luck extended wise counsel over the years to Mike and his family, who were dealing with a wide variety of challenges in the big city.

Up until his death in February 1994, Dr. Luck led a dedicated and distinguished career as an orthopedic surgeon and medical trailblazer. He lives on in a special kind of immortality reserved for people who genuinely care about humanity. An autographed photograph of Dr. Albert Schweitzer hung on Dr. Luck's office wall at the Los Angeles Orthopedic Hospital, where he was medical director from 1955 until 1968.

Dr. Luck's professional achievements were monumental. He invented the Luck Bone Saw, which is used in surgeries around the world. He wrote textbooks on bone and joint disease, pioneered the reattachment of severed limbs and taught in medical schools in addition to performing surgery every day.

The big decision

In 1961, a man named Robert Orona was involved in a construction accident on a Los Angeles freeway. Orona's left arm was nearly severed from his shoulder. In those days, such a massive injury would have usually required amputation. But Dr. Luck decided to try and reattach the appendage, with all its crushed and mangled bones, blood vessels and muscle tissue. The operation on Robert Orona was one of the first successful limb reattachments in medical history.

Mike visited Dr. Luck on dozens of occasions at his hospital office for quiet talks about philosophy, ethics and values. Dr. Luck had a clear vision of cosmic questions such as: *Who are we? Where did we come from? Where are we going?*

It was during one of these heart-to-heart conversations that Dr. Luck disclosed he had originally become interested in orthopedics and medicine in general when his mother's leg was amputated because of an abscess in the knee. Dr. Luck described his purpose in life was to be a good doctor— to solve orthopedic problems. He felt a strong desire to give something back. Above all else, he wanted to care and to serve—and he did, in extraordinary fashion.

Successful modeling

Mike asked Dr. Luck's son, Dr. James V. Luck Jr., while he was still in college, who he most admired in the world and who he would most like to emulate. Jim immediately answered, "My dad," without giving it a second thought. As a tribute to his father's legacy, Jim went on to become medical director and chief executive officer of the same orthopedic hospital in Los Angeles.

Dr. Luck and his wife, Ramona, hosted many dinners, parties and other gatherings in their home to support charitable causes. Their caring activities reached far and wide into dozens of worthwhile causes. From them, Mike received quite an education in the importance of participating in your community.

Good practices get noticed

The executive development portion of the OD program at Disney used to open with each class member giving a personal profile of his or her background, hobbies, talents, family and children. One such day in 1966, one OD class member who worked for the company in Miami reported that his son was a hemophiliac. The Disney employee told the group what a challenge his son's condition posed for the family and how difficult it was to live with the disease day in and day out.

He expressed frustration at how people hardly understood just how high a price families pay when a child requires extensive medical attention. The man went on to say he had been looking forward to the OD session in Los Angeles because there was a doctor in town who was making significant progress in performing surgery on hemophiliacs. The man didn't expect to meet the famous doctor, but he did hope to attend a lecture.

Mike asked the man what the doctor's name was.

"Dr. Vernon Luck of the Los Angeles Orthopedic Hospital," he replied.

Mike didn't let on that he knew Dr. Luck at that point. Instead, Mike called Dr. Luck and asked if he could bring the entire OD group over to visit the hospital. True to his character, Dr. Luck graciously agreed, and a few days later, the group had lunch at the hospital as Dr. Luck's guests. The destination of the field trip that day was not disclosed in advance. Even when the small caravan of cars pulled into the hospital parking lot, the man from Miami didn't pick up on where he was.

The father of the hemophiliac son lit up like a Christmas tree when he saw Dr. Luck approaching us in the waiting room. Dr. Luck's face beamed as he welcomed us. Mike introduced Dr. Luck to the speechless man. It was a moving experience to see the admiration this man had for the doctor.

Dr. Luck invited the group to tour the children's wing of the hospital, which Disney contributions had helped to build. The Doctor told the group he had recently made a plaster cast of Walt's hands because he was studying the hands of famous artists. He intended to give a copy of the cast to Mrs. Disney. The plaster cast was eventually bronzed and housed, we were told, at the California Institute of the Arts.

Pride by association

As Dr. Luck led the OD group through the children's wing, the Disney people were proud to see Disney characters covering almost every square inch of wall space.

Dr. Luck next took the man from Florida by the arm and led him to the room of a hemophiliac patient who had been in surgery only the day before. Dr. Luck asked if anyone in the group had seen the operation written up in the newspaper that morning. He gave the patient some kind and reassuring words, then turned and addressed the OD group.

"We have to be sensitive to human needs," he said, "because this enables us to invent solutions to take care of their needs. When I was a young surgeon, I noticed oil running into an open wound from the bone saw we were using at the time. I was troubled about what I saw and set out to enclose the motor in glass that could withstand the temperatures of the sterilizer. It's called the Luck Bone Saw, and it's used in surgeries all over the world.

"None of us work alone when we're making usable inventions. We depend on each other. That's why I try to build an atmosphere of collaboration and teamwork. This fosters a caring spirit. Consequently, our patients now have a fighting chance."

As we returned from our visit, the Disney employee from Florida was inspired, to say the least. Dr. James Vernon Luck is a tremendous role model for anyone who came into contact with him. He was a truly fantastic human being who offered hope to others in a troubled world. He exemplified a caring spirit by the way he lived his life. He left a legacy of love, devotion and innovation.

The creative principle at work in Dr. Luck's life was being sensitive to human needs, and he strove to invent solutions to meet those needs. Dr. J. Vernon Luck's best practices included:

- Collaboration.
- Teamwork to foster caring.
- Scientific discipline.
- Experimentation.
- Dedication.
- Human interest.
- Spirituality.
- Devotion to excellence.

CHAPTER 6

MICORBS: the seven-step format to break out of the box

MICORBS is a mnemonic for the creative phases of project development. This structure ensures that the proper steps for project implementation are planned in advance, rather than in the middle of the process. Once again, MICORBS stands for:

Master Plan
Idea Development
Communication
Organization
Retrieval
Briefing Boards
Synapse

Displayed Thinking, an enhanced version of storyboarding, is a visual method of thinking. It's helpful to understand that thinking out of the box requires a visual way to think to get the best results. By visualized thinking, we mean getting your ideas up and displayed on boards where they can be expanded and developed by combining them with other ideas and moving them through the creative thinking process. It is an "eyes-on" experience. As we mentioned in Chapter 5, creativity flourishes in an organized environment. The MICORBS sequence organizes the projects for productive creative thought, development and implementation.

The Master Plan

The Master Plan, the first step of MICORBS, is an overview of total project objectives, requirements and deliverables. It provides the foundation upon which everything else is built. The Master Plan details the outline required to reach a specific desired end result. It drives idea development and provides overall control on a project. The Master Plan is a road map to achieving your mission.

The Master Plan board will continue to change and be reshaped as the project evolves. Someone on the team should always be responsible for keeping the Master Plan in front of the group. The Master Plan should be readily visible. It shouldn't be put away in a drawer like a business plan and forgotten. The Master Plan should remain on display, ideally in a Team Center, to be most effective.

Idea Development

Idea Development involves fully expanding on a concept or idea generated by the Master Plan. The ideas from the Master Plan are displayed on a titled Idea Development board. The posting of ideas is the essence of Displayed Thinking. One team member should be assigned the responsibility of seeing to it that ideas are fully detailed and developed.

Communication

Communication is essential to express the details of a major project, event or activity. The communication plan often asks and answers the questions:

- Who needs to know?
- What do they need to know?
- When do they need to know it?
- What media best communicate the information?

The Communications Board can later be used as a checklist to ensure that communications are being carried out. A team member should be assigned the responsibility of making sure the proper communications are being made. Good communication ensures total participation, involvement and understanding.

Organization

Organization is necessary to ensure none of the details are being neglected. Implementation of a project requires organizing details so nothing will slip through the cracks. The Organization plan is the arms and legs of the project and answers the questions:

- What needs to be done?
- Who is going to do what?
- When does it need to be completed?
- What are the required training and development strategies?

Someone on the team must be assigned to keep the Organization board up-to-date and accurate. Roles might shift from time to time, and those changes must be immediately documented to avoid confusion and mistakes. Ron Mannix, chairman and CEO of Loram Corporation in Calgary, often challenges his people to get tuned up and organized.

Retrieval

Retrieval is a method of capturing past or unused ideas and other work on projects that might not have made it into the final mix. Just because an idea isn't right for a certain project doesn't mean it can't be valuable for another. Retrieval of historical and intellectual ideas can be the launching pad for generating fresh ideas and building upon work previously done. Some companies have artifact centers or archives to keep ideas from being lost. The Walt Disney Company and Maytag not only have archives but full-time archivists. A team member must be assigned to make sure no information is lost and that other important information can be accessed. With today's sophisticated electronic microprocessor storage, there's no reason to lose an idea.

Briefing Board

A Briefing Board is the visible during-the-fact control system that allows an individual or team to communicate and organize daily activities. Briefing Boards are organized into five basic areas: Do, Doing, Done, Input and Hang-ups.

Things to do are just that—tasks that need to be accomplished. Things being done are in process. The doing report keeps people abreast of progress. What's completed is posted as done, keeping people informed at a glance. Other people who view the Briefing Boards can post their input on a Briefing Card for you to see. Anyone who has a concern about the project can put their thoughts on a Briefing Card and place it under the Hang-ups to be addressed.

Briefings create assignments requiring action. They provide a quick and effective technique for communicating details on a daily basis. Once again, a team member should be responsible for keeping the Briefing Board current. Briefing Boards, when used properly, can replace many meetings and reports, and they can be easily replicated on electronic information networks.

Synapse

Finally, the Synapse is used to generate ideas by intentionally bringing together seemingly unrelated ideas into meaningful relationships. Pieces of fruitful ideas are often in front of us. Unless we purposefully connect unconnected ideas, we may never reveal valuable relationships and partnerships. Someone on the team needs to periodically facilitate the synaptic process with the team to make sure vital connections are not being lost. Synapse will help the team create synergy, original thinking and breakthrough to better ideas. Synapse not only the ideas within your project and through archival retrieval, but also with concurrent projects.

The five basic applications of MICORBS

It's important to put the MICORBS applications into action. Without action, our efforts will lead to the same nowhere that meaningless meetings lead to. The MICORBS difference is in producing results. The five steps to follow are:

1. **Think visually** and in MICORBS categories. MICORBS helps you to visualize the project phases and to organize the thought process. This approach encourages comprehensive thinking. When envisioning a project, immediately begin organizing your thoughts in terms of Master Plan, Idea Development, Communication, Organization, Retrieval, Briefing Boards and Synapse.

2. **Organize a physical space** to accommodate your organization's Displayed Thinking. Leaders need to think in terms of Team Centers. Set aside space for all seven formats. Look at your current meeting rooms and determine if they're fertile ground for creative thinking and project development.

3. **Organize a project** using the MICORBS applications. When we set up the first Team Center at General Electric, we had a specific problem we addressed very successfully using MICORBS. Using the MICORBS applications is a purposeful act. The MICORBS phases help ensure thorough project development and implementation.

4. Team assignments are critical. Each member of the team needs a function. The leader must know the team members' skills and abilities to make proper assignments.

Most business teams today are thrown together with no thought as to what position each player will play. We recommend seven-person teams to match up with the MICORBS functions. This approach helps ensure productivity and involvement. We recommend limiting the number of people on the team to the number of functions required.

These functions become part of an individual's job description. Team building is an art—a craft that requires planning and forethought. If you're an entrepreneur starting a new business, you might have to play all these roles yourself.

5. Exigency planning means being prepared to deal with emergencies or crises. When the product Tylenol was laced with a deadly chemical, the manufacturer acted immediately and actually improved sales over the following year.

Categorical thinking and the MICORBS applications prepare your organization to move swiftly and effectively when the unexpected strikes. A bumble bee leader and his or her organization are not bogged down in meaningless activities when the need arises for a rapid response.

When leadership begins thinking and functioning in this fashion, the organization will grow and develop as never before. As you'll see in a moment, increasing productivity and profitability are not the only reasons to adopt new project development methods and functions. New technologies and rapidly changing workplaces and marketplaces demand new project organization functions.

New work forms and team types

The type of creative activities represented by the MICORBS applications calls for new boundaryless work forms:

- The virtual team.
- The professional team.
- The individual.

Businesses and other organizations have gone overboard with the idea of teams. Unfortunately, the nature of teams and their best uses are mostly misunderstood. We mentioned earlier that teams are usually assembled without any concept of how a team needs to be structured and facilitated. *Fortune* magazine ran a story about the backlash against teams. Many CEOs and other policymakers are beginning to resist the team concept because they've had too little success with it. Of course, the problem is in the execution of the team approach, not the concept itself. Some overzealous leaders commit to teams without any practical knowledge of how best to use them. When one team fails because of lack of structure and technique, leaders immediately form another team to investigate why the prior team didn't work. The worst scenario of all is when organizations miss their breakthroughs because the proper team systems and procedures aren't in place to capture the solutions when they arise. Undisciplined efforts will invariably result in solutions being overlooked. Incredible ideas drift off into oblivion or are buried along with the trash when teams aren't operating in a structured, disciplined way. We don't want to foolishly miss our breakthrough opportunities because we didn't know how to operate teams properly.

A good leader ought to be able to determine whether a project needs a team or an individual, and then select the kind of team that can best handle it. No one individual is usually smart enough or talented enough to do what an effective team is capable of doing—given the right tools, leaderships and recognition. On the other hand, some tasks could be accomplished by an individual rather than a team, eliminating the waste of time and energy. One of the decisions today's leaders must make is: Should the new team be a virtual team or pro team, or should an individual receive the assignment?

We help leaders in our work by teaching them how to facilitate a team, so as not to be stumbling along trying to make decisions without knowing the different types of teams.

The virtual team

A virtual team is a team assembled for the purpose of solving a problem or identifying a solution as fast as possible. The virtual team gets in contact with the necessary resources. Once the problem has been solved, the team is disbanded. Technology allows the virtual team to meet anywhere, anytime. The key to the virtual team is its quick-hitting nature and rapid-fire solutions. The virtual team is a SWAT team, so to speak.

The professional team

The professional team is assigned to longer-term projects and issues. The members of the pro team receive more training related to their assignment. The mistake that many organizations make is to establish a team to plan a project, only to have another team come in and run it. It reminds us of the old adage "Don't change horses in the middle of the stream." In this case, it's "Don't change teams in the middle of the project."

Where's the ownership and involvement in that approach? If a team knows from the start that its efforts must be deliverable and it is responsible for the long-term implementation and accountability, a whole different attitude pervades the process.

The individual

Peter Drucker's classic book *Management* had been the seminal text for business leadership up until the current technological revolution. In his book, Drucker described the classic divisions of leadership, planning, control, staffing, budgeting, etc. Now technology, advancing at unprecedented speed, is cutting through the old layers. The functional information routes from layer one through layer two through layer three, and so forth, can be bypassed. Anybody can be hooked up to anybody else, anywhere in the universe. Communication time has been slashed.

The idea of boundaryless cultures, originally put into practice by Jack Welch at General Electric, means removing barriers or partitions between layers of the hierarchy or between departments. Once you open up these walls, the people who were once segregated from one another vertically or horizontally can become cross-functional. Rapidly advancing technology has, in many situations, outpaced leadership's ability to properly take advantage of it.

MICORBS provides the structure and content necessary to effectively lead organizations in a high-technology world. MICORBS is the track people run on.

The individual and the phantom team

Thanks to rapidly advancing technology, individuals have never been more powerful than they are today. Individuals can easily access more information and resources from hundreds of databases and libraries. Technology makes job sharing possible. An individual can now assemble a virtual team of virtually any size for virtually any task at virtually any time.

The phantom team is a different concept. It is the team we all carry around with us, made up of our total life experiences, encounters with others and knowledge of the philosophies, strategies and methods of others. The formation of a strong phantom team is one of the best arguments for being a good student—reading, traveling and gathering a broad range of knowledge.

Mike, through his experiences with such great minds as Walt Disney, Buckminster Fuller and others, has gained insight into their thinking and unique approaches to creativity. He draws upon the experience of his phantom team often. Our phantom team is ever-changing, continuing to grow and strengthen as we gather new knowledge and experiences.

The individual as internal consultant

With the partitions coming down between departments, individuals are able to contribute their expertise to a variety of teams and projects. As a roaming resource provider, the individual can be recognized for his or her unique knowledge and skills. Technology has increased flexibility, and the internal consultant can be a valuable resource to organizations.

The individual as entrepreneur

Capitalizing on the same technology that allows individuals to assemble phantom teams and access endless resources and information, the man or woman with a burning desire to invent new products, services and/or processes is free to do so. Of course, old, rigid hierarchical organization charts block creativity and expansive thinking, so the environment and culture must be addressed if organizations expect to unleash the tremendous creative and innovative potential already on the payroll.

New working tasks (and breaks)

The new tasks that accompany the new project development phases and new team styles are the same projects, programs, celebrations and individual activities we described in Chapter 5. What we haven't told you about yet are new types of breaks. The old-fashioned coffee break is a practice that we are now expanding on. We include it on our list along with other new forms.

1. The coffee break. Have a cup of coffee or tea. Eat a donut or Danish. This break is meant to relax you and provide a socializing opportunity.

2. A participation break. Modern technology can have the effect of isolating people. Break time is a good opportunity to get people involved with one another. Once a day or maybe once a week, everybody in the company should work on a single project for at least 15 minutes to keep them mutually informed and involved.

3. The recreation break. For health reasons, it never hurts to get people's blood pumping. This isn't a new idea. From as early as the 1930s, Disney Studio employees were encouraged to play table tennis, basketball, jog or be otherwise physically active during breaks. (During the Herbert Hoover administration, the White House physician invented a new game and ordered the President and his cabinet members to play it every day on the White House lawn. The game was simply volleyball, played with a medicine ball. Hoover Ball tournaments are held annually in West Branch, Iowa, to this day.)

4. A communications break. A major briefing at least once a day with members of the organization will clear people's heads. It's a time for talking openly about all issues that affect employees. This is a scheduled opportunity to let it all out. This type of break often eliminates gossip and the subversive aspects of the grapevine.

5. The learning break. Ideal for the learning organization, the learning break can consist of an internal company talk show or an in-house seminar where valuable subjects are taught.

6. A meditation break. Taking regular quiet and peaceful retreats is extremely important to revitalize personal energy and thought. Some companies have special rooms with dimmed lights and peaceful music where their people can detox from the rigors of the routine.

New job skills

Essential to a successful team effort are job skills, social skills and character development. The job skills relate to specific knowledge, abilities and credentials. Knowing how to pilot the ship, fly the airplane, conduct open-heart surgery, design the skyscraper and so on requires competent job skills.

We've mentioned before that everyone on the team needs to have a role to play. By the same token, somebody on the team has to have some background and knowledge in what you're trying to do. When Card Walker assigned one of Mike's OD teams the task of working on ideas for the entrance complex for the EPCOT Center in Florida, he asked if any of them had ever built a geodesic dome. None of the team members had any experience with geodesic domes, and that's when Mike approached Buckminster Fuller, inventor of the structure. Major point: Always have at least one person on the team who knows what they are doing.

Most existing training and development resources deal with job skills and competency. However, rapidly changing technology is causing the nature of job skills to change at a staggering rate. Job skills training is an ongoing process, to say the least.

Because team efforts are collective endeavors, social skills are extremely important. Knowing how to present ideas, how to defend your position without threatening others and generally working in concert with others is essential to competent teamwork. Many teams today fail because nobody gave any thought to the social skill level of the team members. You can't simply assume that any group of people you throw together is going to have the social skills to work together. Social skills training is virtually nonexistent on the organizational landscape, and yet lack of social skills is a major stumbling block in many organizations.

Just knowing how to converse with others is a problem for many people. Effective team members need to be deipnosophists—they must know how to engage in small talk as well as communicate essential content. Poor social skills can mean chaos. As we've already pointed out, chaos diffuses creative energy. Order and structure focus creative energy—despite what some experts might say—and give us time to break out of the box, just as creativity comes from well-organized environments.

We recommend selecting a diverse team with a variety of social types for thoroughness and flexibility. Issues of character are becoming increasingly important as traditional social ethics distinctions become vague. The more mobile and flexible organizations become, the greater the need to recognize people for who they are, rather than simply what they specialize in. A good, honest person with solid ethical values and a strong work ethic is worth more in the long run than a talented specialist without regard for the rights or feelings of others. The need for training in ethicism is more important now than it's ever been. Long-term success relies heavily on doing right by your employees and your customers.

Thinking out of the box requires new team types, new job skills, social skills and character development, in addition to the MICORBS phases and Displayed Thinking techniques. Creative thinking is considerably more than just sending out a memo and ordering everyone to become creative. It takes the right environment, a supportive culture and attention to techniques, skills and abilities. Recognizing the different types of teams and the realities of team functions and personalities is vital to our success.

Each of these considerations for success is encompassed in the nine-point formula for success, $I^3 + P^3 > C^3$. You cannot leave any part of the formula out or the benefits are likely to fall short. The formula is not difficult to comprehend or apply, but each of the parts must be adapted if we expect the people in our organizations to think out of the box.

Dr. R. Buckminster Fuller:
Product

Buckminster Fuller was a friend to us in many ways, especially in opening our minds to wider horizons. Bucky had the rare ability to clear up the myopia that often afflicts our creative vision—to cure our psychosclerosis. For us, meeting and working with Bucky radically transformed our minds and split our life calendars into BB and AB—Before Bucky and After Bucky.

When Mike's OD project team was assigned the project of doing some way-out thinking for the Walt Disney World entry complex, it was a stimulating experience searching for unique features and structures to incorporate into the plan. Someone on the team suggested contacting Buckminster Fuller, inventor of the geodesic dome, to assist on the project. The team immediately gathered extensive research on Fuller.

In addition to inventing the geodesic dome, he coined the term and developed the concept of synergetics—the coming together of seemingly unrelated components into meaningful relationships, with the whole behaving independent of the parts. Fuller is also known for the "dymaxion principle"—his revolutionary technological design for getting maximum output from minimum energy. He authored many books in a variety of fields, referring to himself as a "comprehensivist." He was a designer, cosmologist, philosopher, mathematician and architect. Ezra Pound called Fuller "a friend of the universe."

Does anybody really know what time it is?

We first met with Dr. Fuller at a small beach motel in Santa Monica. When Mike called to schedule an appointment with him, Fuller said, "I will be happy to meet with you. I'll see you in one year at the Santa Monica Motel." When Mike asked if they couldn't possibly meet a little sooner, Fuller responded, "One year is right away! What kind of calendar do you use anyway? Don't you believe in timelessness?" Before we actually met him, Buckminster Fuller taught us a lesson about the nature of time.

So, one year later, we arrived at Fuller's efficiency apartment at the Santa Monica Hotel at about 10:30 a.m. on a bright and beautiful day at the beach. Bucky, as he asked to be called, had just returned from flying a dymaxion kite on the beach with two 10-year-olds he had just met. His pant legs were rolled up.

"I'm teaching them a few principles of flight and aerodynamics," he explained. "You learn better at the tug end of a kite. May I make you some tea?"

Over the rim of our tea cups, we surveyed the humble motel suite—sitting room, bedroom, kitchen and breakfast nook. The floor was covered with linoleum that had seen better days. Fuller and his wife, Anne, had been living at that motel for 20 years. The place was filled with stacks of books, magazines, papers, video recording equipment and unfamiliar gadgets everywhere. The Fullers' presence made the small suite seem like an academic research center.

Bucky sat in a comfortable reclining chair, sipping thoughtfully from his tea cup, as we conducted an unforgettable interview with one of the world's most unusual people. Fuller had a profound impact on our thinking at a time when it was needed most. He spoke quietly:

"You never change anything by fighting it; you change things by making them obsolete through superior technology. Telstar replaced 500 tons of transoceanic cable. It used to take us three years to circumnavigate the globe in a wooden-hulled ship. It took three months in a steel ship, 90 minutes in a space capsule and now instantaneously with telecommunications.

"You ask me about creativity? We live in a creative universe. We live in a universe of operating general principles with universal functions. We live in a universe where we are cocreators at the best, but I think that's even stretching the truth.

"Superior methodology is everywhere in the grand design of things. Our task is to be creative detectives by doing some first-class spying on the Creator. Creatively, people play the part of Sherlock Holmes for real.

"I didn't invent the geodesic dome. I discovered it through observing geodesic structures in spores under a microscope. This is why every child needs a microscope to make their own discoveries. You know children no longer need to ask questions of people who don't know the answers. We should establish discovery zones throughout our homes rather than rooms with doors, walls and rules."

The last time we saw Bucky, Mike's children—Vanessa, John and Mark—were with us. We all had a wonderful time together. He was recognized and approached by a number of fans. Unlike other celebrities we've known, Bucky was always gracious with his admirers. On this occasion, Bucky gave us all a valuable geography lesson, carefully explaining his famed dymaxion air/ocean map. In his lesson, we learned that we are not the center of the universe.

Bucky died shortly after this memorable occasion—within a short time of his wife, Anne. This poem was included in their joint memorial service:

> *Eye to eye we are nearer*
> *But we truly enter each other's*
> *metaphysical immortal beings*
> *Only through thought and forever*
> *Only through utterly unselfish love*
> *Self is infinitely lonely*
> *Love is infinitely inclusive*

> —from Bucky's poem, *Nearest*,
> written for Anne, July 16, 1967

Jamie Snyder, Bucky's grandson, and Allegra Snyder, Bucky's daughter, have joined us from time to time and have given us even more insight and understanding into Fuller's works and philosophy. Jamie was cruising with us one evening at Marina Del Rey harbor just as the sun was disappearing over the western horizon.[1] Mike told Jamie that Bucky lives on just like the operating general principles of the universe. Creativity, he went on, lives

---

[1]Bucky would argue that the sun doesn't really "set."

forever, just waiting for us to discover a new methodology. Jamie sentimentally agreed.

Buckminster Fuller's best practices included:

- Uncomplicated, nontheoretical methods.
- General principles of the universe.
- Superior comprehension.
- The dymaxion principle.
- Mathematics.

CHAPTER 7

Nine fundamental questions to get out of the box

Just as creativity is the making of the new or the rearranging of the old in a new way, the opposite of creativity is the tyranny of oughtedness, or doing things because we ought to rather than because it's the best thing to do. The Concept of Nine, which addresses the nine fundamental questions for getting out of the box, is not the same as the nine-point formula for success we have previously presented. The Concept of Nine is a step-by-step process that allows us to ask fundamental questions about a problem or project. Each question helps ensure valid thinking and careful research. While the questions themselves may not be original, they can encourage original thinking.

These nine questions, displayed in the chart on page 142, bring involvement, information, inspiration, people, places, products, caring, cooperation and creativity to life.

Philosophical Foundations	Environmental Issues	Leadership Characteristics and Results
1. Assess the way things *are*. Aristotle's Law of Identity: Something is what it is. A is A.	**2. Seek *realistic* thinking.** No distortion. No bluffing. Informal. No illusions. Be realistic.	**3. See the *vision*.** Dream. Objective. Goal.
4. Ask *why*. Cause/Effect. Socrates Law of Causality. The ability to ask a question about an observed effect and then to be able to give the answer by uncovering and understanding the cause.	**5. Become *change-centered*.** *Tabula rasa*—a clean slate. *Elan vital*—the vital urge.	**6. Tap into *ability*.** Capacity to get things done. Accomplish.
7. Ask *how*. How can something be done about the way things are? Plato's Principle of Influence. Performance.	**8. *Don't sanction incompetence*.** Don't ignore incompetence. Teach how not to be.	**9. *Implementation and action*.** Execute the idea. Implement the solutions and deliverables.

Step 1. Assess the way things *are.*

Before we can change anything, we need to understand current conditions. We must be honest and realistic in our assessments. Aristotle's Law of Identity states, "Something is what it is. A is A." The first question provides a foundation on which all subsequent questions rest. We must have a true picture of the facts and reality of the situation.

There must also be clear criteria to validate input. The goal is a clear understanding of the way things *are.* Aristotle's law of identity, plainly stated, means things are what they are regardless of the perceiver's perception. His law was popularized in the works of Ayn Rand and Victor Hugo.[1] Things are what they are. Call an ace an ace.

Step 2. Seek *realistic* thinking.

When we strive for realism in our endeavors, we employ foresight, imagination, visualization and projecting the vision of what we want to do. Assessing reality requires sensanation, or the use of all five senses. We must also philosophically examine *what is* in terms of existence, being and living.

Realism means avoiding distortion, bluffing and illusions. Distortion is taking A is A and claiming that A is B. Bluffing can include hiding, withholding or burying things. In an environment of bluffing, we will never see reality the way it really is and the conclusions we reach will be flawed. Identifying things as they truly are requires a faithful portrayal of reality. The climate among team members should be favorable if realism is to prevail.

Part of being realistic is being informal. Informal environments rarely get too uptight. By informal we don't mean window-dressing informality, like not wearing a jacket and tie or calling people by their first names. We can practice these surface values and still be rigid and formal in our relationships. The true measure of informality is the freedom to say what we

---

[1]There's a tremendous amount of fine literature about Aristotle available. One of the best is Dr. Mortimer Adler's *Aristotle for Everyone*.

need to say to whomever we need to say it whenever we want without fear of unjust reprisal or power play.

True informality is a rare commodity. Truly informal organizations run circles around formal organizations because the informality ensures freedom to act. Free and unbridled people will outproduce restrained thinkers every time.

Walt Disney believed if you are grounded in reality, then you have the ability to break out and really fly to fantasy. He knew believing in illusions will cause you to crash because your beliefs lack realism. People have trouble going to fantasy if they're bluffing, distorting or covering up. They don't have the freedom fantasy requires.

Realistic environments invariably have an abundance of humor. If humor is the unmasking of the hypocritical, as we've already stated, then it can't coexist with bluffing, distorting or hiding what's going on. High-level creativity and thinking out of the box occur where people are free enough to have fun.

Step 3. See the *vision.*

Vision results from being realistic when assessing the way things are. The term "vision" is sometimes interchanged with "dream." Those who find the term "dream" too saccharine often opt for "objective" or "goal." If you really want to sound serious, use "long-range strategic objective."[2]

One of the characteristics of a vision, based on the way things really are, is its doability. You've heard and used the slang term for unrealistic goals and expectations a million times. They're called pipe dreams. People who peddle pipe dreams are usually accused of blowing smoke. You can almost see the smoke trailing behind some people as they walk. Unrealistic people stir up a lot of dust, but produce very little action.

Dreams become doable when they are grounded in reality. Objectives and goals become attainable. Vision is borne from realism, and realism

---

[2]Terms like "long-range strategic objective" are particularly popular among those types who have spent time together in the wilderness, sliding down cables and shooting each other with paint pellets. In the end, visions, dreams, goals and objectives are actually the same. What matters most is what we want to achieve.

develops from objectively observing life around us. Vision is part of the nine-part formula discussed in Chapter 3.

Step 4. Ask *why.*

Why are things the way they are? What are the causes and effects? What are the motivations behind current conditions? Looking at things the way they are reveals the effect. When you ask yourself the question "Why is that so?", you're asking the fundamental question. We can't think out of the box without first asking the fundamental question. The fundamental question will always relate to an effect we're observing and the cause behind it.

Socrates' Law of Causality addresses the ability to ask a question about an observed effect and then to give the answer by uncovering and understanding the cause.[3] A physician, for example, observes effects—or symptoms—in a patient and can then diagnose the cause—a specific condition or disease. Realistic thinking identifies the cause of a symptom, which enables the physician to create a plan—a vision—for treatment.

Step 5. Become *change-centered.*

A change-oriented person does not resist change. After ascertaining the cause, a change-centered person will seek to alter the effect. A great many people appear to resist change, but, as previously discussed, they're really just disappointed by previously unfulfilled promises of change. What seems to be resistance is really fear of another disappointment.

A change-centered person likes the idea of *tabula rasa.* He or she wants to have a blank page or open mind on which to sketch and create something that will make a difference. *Tabula rasa* fosters *elan vital,* or the vital urge, which stimulates us to act. Improvement comes through altering, modifying and transforming. New solutions shouldn't be bound up by old thinking.

---

[3]Among the many books on Socrates, we most recommend Thelma Levine's *From Socrates to Sartre.* Dr. Levine is a professor of philosophy at Georgetown University.

Step 6. Tap into *ability.*

Ability is the capacity to get things done. The capacity to accomplish is further defined by coming to closure on the issues and offering solutions. Getting things accomplished requires the skilled use of resources. People can accurately assess the way things are and envision new ideas, but without the ability to successfully act on their ideas, nothing really changes. This is one of the strongest arguments for fostering a learning environment. This is why training and development should be top priority.

Step 7. Ask *how.*

The concept

How can something be done about the way things are? Recall when Mike taught his son about the nine dots. They discussed the concept behind the exercise.

First, we must understand the concept behind an issue. Effective leaders and teachers explain a concept repeatedly to ensure comprehension. Coaches will often explain to their teams, "Here's what we're trying to do." Second, we must share clear and easy-to-understand examples that illustrate the concepts.

The example

Great pedagogy, great teachers, great leaders and the people who develop spectacular products rely on the use of examples. Their techniques revolve around exhaustively demonstrating concepts through illustrations and examples. When Mike described the concept behind the nine dots to his son, John, he explained the concept of an imaginary box. Mike further explained how he could project himself outside the box to find his solution. The example was to start showing him how to do it without going too far. In essence, Mike gave John a model. The worst thing Mike could have done was to give him the answer outright.

We often unwittingly teach our children to be dependent upon authority to give them the answers. Children learn early on to do what the authority figure wants—the way the authority figure wants it done.

Parents, baby sitters, teachers, bosses—it's no wonder people are reluctant to act autonomously and self-direct themselves. If there's no authority figure around to give them the answer, they're stuck. The whole idea of codependence is alive and well in leadership today. The fact people need leaders to give them the answers or approve every move they make or set strict policies that stifle creativity and control behavior fits the cycle of dependency. This is fading out. For example, the outstanding headmaster of Flintridge Preparatory School in California, Peter Bachman, doesn't dictate policy at his school but encourages full student and faculty participation in problem-solving. He presents concepts and gives examples.

Step 8. *Don't sanction incompetence.*

One of the reasons we have so much incompetence in the world is that we ignore it and walk away. Incompetence is often rationalized as inevitable, inescapable or merely "the way it is." We can't have vision if we avoid confronting and correcting incompetence.

Sanctioning incompetence means acquiescing to the status quo. If we really want to make positive changes, we must know what we're doing and have consent to take the necessary risks. Selecting the right people to do the right job and exposing them to constant information and education will eliminate harmful lack of knowledge.

If we're willing to confront incompetence, we have to teach people how not to be incompetent. That means committing the time and resources to help people develop the skills they need. We should be patient and employ constructive criticism. The learning organization is constantly developing people, at every level, as part of the day-to-day operation of the organization. Training and development isn't relegated to a human resources department in another building but is everyone's concern.

To ignore and walk away from incompetence is to sanction it. That's why we crusade to help people understand and get the education and training they need to be successful.

If leaders expect their teams to be competent, leaders must deal with their own incompetence first and lead by example. Anyone who has worked with us, from big companies to little startup businesses, has heard us emphasize the concept of incompetence. Time and time again, we see organizations that don't apply proper methodology to team functions. There's enough chaos to manage without creating more.

Otherwise competent people are rendered creatively impotent by chaotic, unstructured team assignments and environments. This gets translated as incompetence—and it occurs in all sorts of environments. For example, one evening at a hotel, Mike put in a request for a wake-up call for 6:30 a.m. The operator said, "Could you wake up at 6:45 a.m.?" Mike asked why. The operator replied, "There are too many people waking up at 6:30 a.m." Mike asked, "When do you want me to wake up?" The operator replied, "We have an opening at 6:45 a.m." It was late at night so Mike said, "Okay." However, the operator called him at 6:30 a.m. the next morning anyway. Mike said, "I'm not waking up."

In our work, we constantly fashion training and education programs, ideas and examples to encourage and facilitate growth and development in people. The historical accomplishments of The Walt Disney Company are examples of what enlightened organizational development should be about. Walt didn't tolerate incompetence. Neither should any of us. Disney earned its world-class reputation for excellence based, in large part, on the ceaseless dedication to education and training. Blindness to incompetence, or the inability to detect it, is in and of itself incompetent.

Step 9. *Implementation.*

The final fundamental question is how to implement our vision—to take action, to make it happen. The leadership characteristic of implementing, or carrying through to closure, is based on the ability to produce deliverables. The ability to rally sufficient people and resources to put an idea into practice is an essential leadership characteristic.

One of the most frustrating experiences in life is getting to the goal line and failing to score—making it to the altar and not getting married. Delivering the deliverables is based on the successful execution of the fundamentals that precede implementation.

Implementation and action are accomplished most effectively when each of the steps is completed. Review the chart on page 142.

Enriched places

Many of the ideas in the nine fundamental questions are based on the philosophies of the ancient Greek scholars. They're time-honored principles, well-tested through the centuries. The enriched places that Frank Lloyd Wright talked about and Walt Disney understood so well are rooted in ancient Greece. The Team Center had its origins in Aristotle's Lyceum, a learning center/gathering place. Socrates had the Paideia Center, which means, in Greek, the bringing up of the child and the educating of the person. Before Aristotle had his Lyceum, he was a student at Plato's Academy, which was the forerunner of our modern universities. We urge every organization to establish an academy. Even if you're a one-person startup, you can hook up with online services and form your own virtual academy.

The basic logic in the nine fundamental questions for thinking out of the box comes from valid data. When we're creating ideas, we pose these questions. The deeper we inquiry, the more useful the answers will be. The more honest the answers, the more powerful our solutions. The nine fundamental questions might be composed as follows:

1. "What *are* things really like?" (Identify the need.)
2. "*Why* are they the way they are?" (The cause behind the effects.)
3. "*How* are we going to change?" (Concepts and examples.)
4. "Is our plan *realistic* and deliverable?" (Logical and valid.)
5. "Are we really *change*-oriented?" (Open and willing.)
6. "Do we *sanction incompetence*?" (Don't ignore the problems.)
7. "Have our ideas been formed into a *vision*?" (The goal or objectives, with a method.)

8. "Do we have people on the team with *ability*?" (Experience, education and training.)
9. "Are we prepared to see this thing through to the end?" (*Implementation* and action.)

The dirt mover example

When Walt Disney World was being built in Florida, literally everyone—thousands of people who worked on the site—were required to attend two days of training on the Disney philosophy. Even if some subcontractors had only a few days of work, they were paid for two additional days to attend the sessions on the Disney Way. Roy O. Disney believed strongly in building the Disney philosophy into the very foundation of the facility. Even if a customer would never see the way foundations were poured or how well the wiring was done, Disney quality went into the foundation.

A very large man who operated a bulldozer came to one of Mike's sessions at Walt Disney "U." The dirt mover had no expertise except to move dirt. He was clearly unhappy about attending this long seminar. He sat in the front row, slumped in his chair, scratching, chewing and spitting tobacco, smoking and snorting snuff throughout the two-day session.

After the seminar was finished, the man came up to Mike and said something surprising: "I enjoyed your seminar. Not right away. I went home the first night hating you. You used big words, words like 'epistemology.' You knew I didn't understand big words but you used them anyway. I didn't understand half of what you said. But, I enjoyed it anyway. You didn't treat me like I was dumb. Thank you. Please tell Mr. Disney I appreciate being invited. Nobody's ever invited me to nothing before. I'll move the dirt really good."

Mike did one better than carry a message to Roy Disney; he took the man to meet him. Roy was a small man. His eye level was about at the dirt mover's belt buckle. Roy welcomed the man warmly, as if they were eyeball to eyeball, and asked what the man did. The dirt mover replied, "I move dirt." Roy thought a moment and said, "So do I. I work with bankers. It's the same thing." Roy invited the man to join him in a cup of coffee and a piece of pie. A pot of coffee and a whole pie later they finished their conversation.

Mike complimented the man on admitting to what he didn't know. Nobody knows everything. No matter how enthusiastic we get in our work—and we get pretty enthusiastic—it doesn't mean we think we know it all. We've found that most of the people who think they know all the answers usually have very few of the answers. The true mark of a learning organization is broad acceptance that there is always more to learn.

Not only did the dirt mover move dirt at Walt Disney World like he had never moved dirt before, news of Roy's coffee klatsch spread like wildfire throughout the organization. There was a tremendous sense of team spirit. That's why we drill the fundamentals so hard and hammer home the importance of attention to detail. The process is important, and people are important. The way the dirt mover moved dirt affected the quality of the foundation upon which buildings and attractions were built. What he did was extremely important. To exclude him from the team would have been foolish and unrealistic.

Who builds foundations for your organization? Who maintains the environment? Who makes sure information is passed on and processed? Everybody has a role to play. If they don't, what are they on the payroll for? If they have a role to play, they need to feel part of what's going on. More importantly, everyone needs to know and understand what role they're playing. Otherwise, how can you encourage them to grow and develop and excel? Never talk down to anyone or minimize their contributions.

Thinking out of the box is, in part, a structured, disciplined endeavor. As you now know, the creative-thinking process has elements of a free-for-all and unbounded exchange of ideas. However, the Displayed Thinking process as a whole is a systematic journey that not only stimulates creative ideas, but also captures them. The Concept of Nine applies to you, your organization and whatever challenge lies ahead.

A.C. (Mike) Markkula: Caring

*"We couldn't have accomplished what we did
at Apple without the help of Mike Vance."*

A.C. (Mike) Markkula, founder and chairman of Apple Computer, made that statement at the 1992 Creative Thinking Association of America awards banquet in Las Vegas. Mike was so moved by the unexpected and generous compliment he missed his next cue. Markkula is one of the people he respects most. The two worked together extensively during the startup years of Apple Computer.

We include Markkula in this list because he exemplifies an attitude of caring. He's what AT&T executive Robert Greenleaf calls in his book, *Servant Leadership,* a basically good man. Indeed, Mike Markkula is a basically good man who does what's right instead of what's politically expedient.

Making more of people

Mentoring comes naturally to Mike Markkula. He makes people be more than what they are, not through superficial techniques, but by setting a superlative example. He makes people work harder at outstanding and worthwhile accomplishments. Markkula is a low-key, very private man. We run the risk of embarrassing him in this profile. He's simply not motivated by gaining popularity or recognition. He doesn't seek the limelight or strive to be a "big man." He is a big man by the very nature of his character.

Mike Vance and Mike Markkula have had a number of meaningful conversations since they've known and worked with each other. One such conversation took place during a break from an Apple training seminar in 1978. The two sat in Markkula's Porsche outside the Quail Lodge in Carmel, California, discussing Aristotle, Plato, Socrates and the origins of Western thought and civilization. Mike Vance had spoken all day to about 50 people who represented the Apple startup cadre. Discussing the old Greeks helped put them in the right frame of mind to consider the question foremost on Markkula's mind at that time—Apple Values.

The values discussion began in earnest and became increasingly intense as the two men talked for hours. During this Porsche meeting, Markkula said, "Integrity is more important than techniques. Good values are our greatest asset. We must build Apple Values into something unmatched by anyone. Values are everything. We've got to get that message through. It's like your point about incompetence."

What Markkula was referring to is the importance of not sanctioning or ignoring incompetence. Markkula added that service continues to decline, in part, because customers accept it without so much as a whimper. That's what we mean by no values. If you take values seriously, you will have good standards to uphold. Good standards and values made Disneyland the unprecedented success it has become.

Markkula went on: "We just want Apple to be different. We want to build great values and make damn sure we never lose sight of them."

We had a stimulating lunch with Mike again at the Fairmont Hotel in San Francisco in 1990. Once again we had a wonderful time philosophizing, reminiscing, dreaming and talking about his new projects. We were glad to hear of his involvement in an Ethics Foundation study, as well as a project on brain imprinting and mapping. We all agreed that "management by values" would be the primary leadership paradigm for the future.

Creativity flourishes where there is integrity. Markkula said, "Integrity is more important than techniques. Good values are our greatest asset." Mike Markkula's best practices include:

- Engineering.
- Ethics.
- Collaboration.
- Public service.
- Mentoring.
- Realism.

CHAPTER 8

Ideation techniques

The creative thinking techniques you learned in Chapter 7 will help you think out of the box. The ideation techniques you're about to learn will help you *break* out of the box. Ideation techniques are principles that can lead to original thinking. The following illustrations, concepts and examples will introduce you to the functional workings for ideation approaches that are very effective.

A common question is, "How can I come up with creative ideas or create something new?" We mentioned earlier that Walt Disney believed the path to riches was to find something no one wants and make it valuable by what you contribute to it. To that thought he added, "Don't copy other people. Create something original, add to or improve on products and services that have already been done."

A group of college students once asked us what they should do in the face of a dwindling job market. We gave them an ideation technique, a development idea about what kind of career they could pursue. Our suggestion was simple: Open the yellow pages directory and put your finger down anywhere. Whatever business you discover under your finger, do to it what Walt Disney said—add to or improve upon it. You'll succeed if you add value to the way the business is currently conducted.

You don't need to rack your brain necessarily trying to find something nobody has ever done before. That's not the point. Just do anything really better than it's ever been done before. Create new methods, benefits and features others haven't even thought of yet. Don't squander your intellectual equity on creating a new product or service if no one wants it. Invest instead on improving upon something that exists by romancing it to a new level of excellence.

A man who took our advice to heart recently reported on his progress. He took an ordinary hairbrush and developed a collapsible hairbrush that fits in the breast pocket of a man's shirt. It's a perfectly functioning hairbrush that fits in the palm of your hand but folds flat with the push of a button. He improved on an old concept in an ingenious way by thinking out of the box. He did to the hairbrush what Walt Disney did to the amusement park. He made it more flexible in function and appealing. Of the many ideation techniques, adding value is the most fundamental.

Idea Creation Matrix

Place	Invention/Inventions	Things
People	Invention/Extensions	Thoughts
Product	Invention/Deinventions	Social Contracts
	Functional Substitutions	

This diagram represents a variety of perspectives through which you can stimulate creative ideas. Some of these concepts (place, people, product) we've discussed at length in previous chapters. But let's take a closer look at the four ideation techniques shown in the middle of the diagram.

1. Invention/Inventions

Some ideas or inventions will require that something else be invented first, before the original concept can be fully realized. For example, Edison invented the incandescent light bulb. But before it could be enjoyed, he had to create a number of other products, such as wiring, switches, sockets, fuses and so forth. The result from his Invention/Inventions system eventually became a company called General Electric.[1]

2. Invention/Extensions

Some inventions can be improved by extending or enhancing the original concept. However, the invention itself is not dependent on the extension to function. The common hairbrush isn't dependent on the collapsible hairbrush to be usable. However, the collapsible hairbrush raises the concept of a hairbrush to another level of usefulness and added portability, sometimes called an improvement, or "plusing." The classic example of an Invention/Extension is the eraser on a pencil. The pencil is the basic invention. Attaching an eraser extends it. A corkscrew with a bottle opener attached at the other end is another example of an Invention/Extensions ideation technique.

3. Invention/Deinventions

Some inventions are "uninvented" for one reason or another. The Star Wars antimissile system for outer space, whether it would have ever worked or not, was an example of an invention to deinvent or render useless an invention of massive destructive power. The bulletproof vest is an invention that, hopefully, reduces the effect of another invention. If you're a soft drink company, you want your product to nearly deinvent another cola company.

4. Functional Substitutions

Some inventions are achieved by replacing one product or idea with one that is better. Telstar, the communications satellite, is an example of

---

[1]General Electric was first called the Edison Electric Company.

functionally substituting one invention for another, since the communications satellite replaces tons and tons of transoceanic wire cable. Early watches used to be handmade—a labor-intensive effort. Now, a mechanized process increases production, lowers costs and increases reliability. Typesetting, for books like this one, is no longer done by an apprentice with an ink-stained apron and hands, one letter or word at a time. Computers have been functionally substituted with vastly improved results and speed.

Invention/Inventions, Invention/Extensions, Invention/Deinventions and Functional Substitutions are each examples of ideation techniques. Imagine you're the skipper of a large ocean-going ship and you order a turn 15 degrees to port, and nothing happens. You ask again for a turn 15 degrees to port and still nothing happens. After asking a third time and still getting no results, you're getting ticked off. It's perplexing because you and your crew have just returned from a seminar on team-building where you had quality time together, bonding and trust-building, but you still can't get your ship turned around for some reason.

As a last resort, you abandon your participative leadership style and shout at your crew to turn the damn ship. Still nothing. Finally, a junior officer, who has just graduated from MIT, speaks up and tells you the rudder on the ship is not capable of making a 15 degree turn to port under the current conditions. Then you realize, no matter how great your leadership is, no matter how correct your procedures are, no matter how many MBAs you have on board—until you design the right rudder, the ship won't turn to satisfy your command.

An important ideation technique is revealed in this illustration. In determining if the rudder must be redesigned to accommodate the maneuver you want to make, you must ask yourself the question, "Is the idea I'm trying to develop doable the way it's currently being proposed?" The question itself embodies the technique. Put another way, you might ask, "Can I force a square peg through this round hole?" In order to make progress, this question must be asked and honestly answered. Only then will you know what your requirements are. To get started, you'll use Powwows, Brainstorming, Mind Boggling and Work Outs. Refer to the chart on page 159 while studying these concepts.

POWWOWS

Purpose:
To get started. An open, friendly session to lay the groundwork. Sit around a fireplace and set the mood for the social and working relationships ahead.

The Goal:
To get acquainted and bond.

Special Techniques:
Start directory of team members' skills, background, interests, etc. Start posting ideas on Master Plan board.

Skills inventory, interests inventory, data dump.

Everyone jumps in. Separate out negatives; form tentative ideas/solutions.

Understand team members' skills and viewpoints.

BRAINSTORMING

Purpose:
To come up with preliminary ideas in a smooth-running, fast-paced atmosphere.

Note:
No confrontation at this point.

Special Techniques:
Displayed Thinking Boards.

Post and defer negatives to a later time so as to not disrupt the rhythm of the session.

Hitchhike ideas on other ideas.

Issues begin to be identified. Still no closure expected.

Very few solutions or breakthroughs, if any.

Continue to develop Master Plan Board. Set up Briefing Board.

MIND BOGGLING

Purpose:
To blow your mind open, to boggle it, to think out of the box, to get hundreds of ideas.

Note:
A wide open madhouse, but much fun is in the doing.

Special Techniques:
Free-flowing to topics, subjects, needs.

Totally open, wild, way-out thinking, no restraints, nothing out of bounds.

Still no closure expected. Very few solutions at this point.

WORK OUTS

Purpose:
To lay everything on the table, work through, debate and come to closure.

Note:
A wide open session. Go at it. Take the gloves off. Most of all...have fun.

Special Techniques:
Detail and develop ideas. Synapse Board is up-to-date. Sorting of the scattered idea cards into pairs or couples. Matrix is formed.

Communications and Organization Boards are created to answer questions for implementation.

Issues and answers, pros and cons, debate and argue, ideas and solutions.

All MICORBS phases have been completed.

Closures and deliverables are expected. Work out all loose ends.

159

The powwow

The powwow is primarily an ice-breaking event, a preliminary opportunity for team members to get to know one another. It was developed when Walt Disney was asked if he liked to conduct brainstorming sessions by an OD group. He responded that he preferred to hold a kind of powwow, where people get together, beat the drum, light a fire, smoke a pipe and socialize. Getting to know one another is the best way to learn what others might contribute to idea development on the team. The purpose of the powwow is to get your team started, but it isn't meant to produce any conclusions.

The powwow technique is intentionally open, friendly, not highly directed or structured, and it is intended to lay the groundwork for the team's working relationship. Powwows can be held in Team Centers, restaurants or some other relaxing atmosphere where you can set a congenial mood. The powwow provides the very important element of socializing. The new methodologies, such as boundaryless cultures, call for successful social interaction. Building social relationships in the workplace is now real work. Social activities are viewed by those in the old school as soft. Some hard-nosed types even consider it goofing off at company expense. The powwow is anything but goofing off. As you're informally getting to know each other, the various issues and divergent viewpoints begin to surface.

The powwow should be acknowledged as a first step in a team-building process—not an end in and of itself. We often tightly structure encounter exercises, but fail to follow up with any structure for the team's actual operations. Getting your team acquainted with one another is a foundation-laying activity. It should be viewed as the real work, not a mere exercise.

The team leader and each team member should pay attention during the powwow and begin cataloging on Displayed Thinking sheets the skills and interests of each team member. Of special importance is the attitude each member of the team displays toward the project. In short, the team needs to develop a profile on each team member. Powwows should have three distinct parts:

1. A skills inventory. Each person describes for the group his or her skills, strengths, experience and demonstrated aptitude, in order to identify resources and strengths that could be called upon during the project. There will always be unique features in the mixture of diverse personalities.

2. An interest inventory. Each person describes to the group what he or she likes to do—activities that may not appear to have anything to do with the project. Some people like to ski, some like to fish, some like to travel. Everyone has unique interests that should be understood and serve as points of fellowship between members.

3. The data dump. In an open and nonthreatening environment, each person expresses his or her thoughts and feelings about the project. In a data dump, the person who has the floor is not interrupted. It's not a discussion. Everyone listens to the speaker until it's someone else's turn to speak.

A good data dump will cut down on some of the complaining that individuals often do when they never get the opportunity to be heard. Expressing their feelings about the topic or project at this time may cut down on the interruptions later. (It's an effective time to use the category note-taking and Displayed Thinking techniques we've mentioned. The knowledge you collect at a data dump speeds the team progress along.)

Powwows give everyone an opportunity to jump in and get involved. The stage is set and the practice of open communication is established. The negatives are brought out and identified. Most important, the creative process is now set in motion. By the end of the powwow, people are already beginning to produce tentative ideas and solutions for the project. They're beginning to think like creative problem-solvers, and a cohesive unit is beginning to take shape.

Special techniques for powwows

It's important to resist the urge to come to solutions at a powwow. Powwows are not designed to produce closure. There are other valuable steps ahead that will produce and refine more ideas and solutions. A powwow might seem like the only technique you'll need to get a problem solved or a new program figured out. Not so. A powwow is important and requires continuous attention, but subsequent exercises are designed to move the creative process toward the goal.

At the powwow you can begin posting ideas on a Master Plan board (the "M" in MICORBS), under subject categories such as "team members," "skills," "data dump" and "miscellaneous."

We recommend setting up your Briefing Board (the "B" in MICORBS) at this time so you can start listing the "to-do's" and project status.

We stress again that without the powwow, you may have difficulties attempting to work together. Just having dinner, drinks, fun and games with each other won't accomplish the goal, but it's the foundation. Powwows need to be completed before work on the project begins. It's discouraging to get into projects and suddenly realize you haven't adequately assessed team members' backgrounds, skills, strengths and interests along with the project data. Don't wait until there is personality conflict. Get a fix on the composition and distinct personality of your team right off the bat—*powwow*.

Brainstorming

We focus on the brainstorming technique at this point because the practice hooks on to the concept of the powwow. Alex Osborne was a pioneer of brainstorming techniques, and most people might think Walt Disney followed suit. Classic brainstorming doesn't allow for negative thoughts or criticism. Typically, it follows three ground rules: 1) No criticism of ideas; 2) No negative thoughts; and 3) Abundance of ideas. However, Walt didn't like the prohibition on negatives and criticism, which are the principle ground rules of brainstorming. Those who worked with him over the years knew he believed ideas and creative thinking resulted from vigorous discussion, struggle and even argument over conflicting points of view, as his working style revealed. In our creative thinking technique sessions, we don't ignore criticisms; we just put them under a "defer status" category. Then, later on, we allot time for analytical thinking and objections countering in order to keep the project balanced and moving.

The primary purpose of brainstorming is to come up with preliminary ideas in a positive, smooth-running atmosphere for the development of the Master Plan. The more ideas, the better. A brainstorming session is fast-paced and "big-picture" in order to stimulate a quick and free flow of ideas. The brainstorming session is not intended to be a time for confrontation from the participants.

Special techniques for brainstorming

When someone throws out an idea, other people might hitchhike on it. The brainstorming session is the time to capture ideas on flip charts or other display boards.[2]

In a free-flowing exchange of ideas, it's not uncommon for team members to find themselves on a tangent not realizing how they got there. That's why tracing helps them work backward to uncover their path. Tracing is especially valuable because it exposes how apparently divergent ideas are connected.

As we mentioned earlier, an additional component of the brainstorming process is the defer status, which allows participants to list the negatives to be dealt with at another time. Just because someone has a negative thought doesn't necessarily mean the thought won't be helpful in some way later. But if you stop the spontaneous flow in order to deal with the negative, the rhythm of the creative process is disrupted. When a negative thought appears, note it and defer it until later so it's not lost and the person who contributed the negative thought won't feel as if his or her thoughts are being discounted.

As with the powwow, solutions or closures should not be expected during the brainstorming sessions. These sessions will produce many kinds of ideas and will begin to identify more issues of importance, continuing to develop the Master Plan and the big picture. As a result, the

---

[2]We prefer using cards in Displayed Thinking because they allow more flexibility for movement.

brainstorming session will produce a few deliverables. You're in no way finished with ideation techniques, but you will begin accumulating some implementable ideas. Many worthwhile ideas are discovered *en route* to the solution of other issues.

Mind boggling

Similar to the mindquake principle we learned from Buckminster Fuller, mind boggling is a deliberate attempt to blow our minds out of the box. Wilder than brainstorming, mind boggling is thinking out of the box like nobody's business. No box can contain a mind boggle. Mind boggling should be a lot of fun. It should be a wide open madhouse. In fact, Walt Disney used to say, "It will be a madhouse," while arching his eyebrow in delight. Be prepared for many possible arguments and confrontations. This is the time to develop and detail the ideas on the Idea Development Boards (the "I" in MICORBS). Handle negatives as you did in brainstorming. Defer them before they become a distracting focus of the session but let them really come out in the open.

Special techniques for mind boggling

When a topic is presented, everyone free-flows to that topic with their ideas. The free flow will produce subjects under the topic, and everyone should let their ideas free-flow to those subjects. Of course, every one of these ideas should be written down and boarded. Capturing the ideas that emerge during any one of these processes is critical to overall success. The free-flowing process produces a great volume of ideas in a somewhat chaotic atmosphere. However, you're prepared in advance for the free-flowing nature of the discussions by making sure everyone writes down and displays their ideas. You don't want to restrict way-out thinking in any way. There are no restraints and nothing is out of bounds in free-flowing.

Like powwows and brainstorming, mind boggling isn't expected to specifically produce closures, even though you will probably get to some deliverables.

The work out

The work out technique was developed and used extensively in developing projects at Disney.

The work out is distinctly different from the other ideation forms, as it's finally the appropriate time for coming to solutions. You address the proposals you've come up with during brainstorming and mind boggling. You debate, work through and come to closure on them. Work outs are the most confrontational form in the ideation exercises and project development. Nothing is held back as you and your team seek to refine and detail ideas and concepts into functional, implementable, deliverable plans. Deliverables and closures are expected. Loose ends should be pulled together, sorted out and tied up by the end of your project's work out.

Special techniques for work outs

During the work out process, we recommend active use of the synapse board (the "S" in MICORBS), where the final sorting of ideas is completed. Start by scattering the ideas everywhere on the board. Then, as relationships between ideas begin to emerge inductively, you put those cards together in pairs or couples. Then you'll begin to make connections where specific pairs or couples belong together naturally. This pairing or coupling leads you to a matrix. The work out matrix will help produce solutions to the problem.

Start your Communications Board (the "C" in MICORBS) and the Organizational Board (the "O" of the MICORBS). These phrases identify the issues that need to be addressed for closure and implementation of a project. The Communications Board answers numerous questions, such as:

- Who needs to know?
- What do they need to know?
- When do they need to know?
- How are we going to communicate it?

The Organizational Board answers numerous questions, such as:

• What needs to be done?
• When does it need to be done?
• Who is going to do it?
• How are they going to do it?

These questions can also be answered and placed on a Time Line or Calendar Board. This displays to everyone all the implementation steps to be completed day-by-day, month-by-month.

There are other issues and details to be spelled out. For instance, what resources will be required? The deliverables in a work out must include a complete list of related issues and answers, pros and cons, debates and arguments, and ideas and solutions.

Sorting is one of the activities engaged in during a work out. Here, the ideas are gathered from as far back as the powwow. You begin to organize ideas you intend to use, as well as store in retrieval (the "R" in MICORBS) ideas you're not going to use right now.

We see companies who have no clue as to how desperately they need to get their people involved and inspired through the proper implementation of these techniques. Learning organizations call for extensive training in this area. If your organization is not engaged in original thinking and developing original products and services, it's probably because these four simple-but-profound ideation techniques are not being correctly used and are not part of a company's corporate culture. Our experience leaves no doubt that attending to these four ideation techniques—and the other creative thinking processes we've described for you—produces great results.

Sex, passion and desire

Other essential ingredients to achieving out-of-the-box thinking go beyond techniques, methods and processes. Mike knew the late western author Louis L'Amour. Louis appeared on Mike's television show "Men at the Top" and joined Mike for lunch at the Disney studios from time to time. A super guy. During one of their mostly philosophical conversations, Mike said to Louis, "You've written so many successful books. Many of them have been made into movies. You're a great example of prolific creativity. What do you think, more than anything else, stimulates and fosters creativity?"

Louis responded by saying, "The issue, Mike, is not whether somebody is creative or not creative. The issue is their motivation."

Mike asked him what he meant by that.

"There are three things that stimulate creativity within you," L'Amour continued, "sex, passion and desire. If you remove sex, passion and desire, creativity dies."

L'Amour was not referring to carnal pursuits or prurient interests. Rather, he referred to a passion for life, stemming from individual convictions and beliefs, emotions and subsequent fervor and zeal. There must be a burning desire to achieve something, stemming from these passions and convictions. Thus, these ideation techniques require a cultural setting in accordance with such convictions. It is these convictions that become catalysts for creativity.

Louis L'Amour believed, as Buckminster Fuller did, that people were not creative, *per se*, but that we live in a universe full of creativity and we simply uncover it. Calling someone creative or naming a department for creativity annoyed Louis because he didn't believe human beings could create creativity. Thomas Edison and Buckminster Fuller believed similarly that we exist in a creative universe and the best we can do is discover preexisting principles that are out there.

Edison went so far as to distinguish between inventing something and discovering it. One of the greatest inventors of all time claimed that he only uncovered things that existed in the universe. If it's not out there, Edison believed, you'll never find it...no matter how creative you think you are. If it's out there, you can find it if you're looking.

The difference between those we call creative and those who don't appear to have a creative bone in their body is motivation. Something must have metaphorical sex appeal to really get us going. We have to feel passionately about life to really do it justice. Without genuine desire, there will be no motivation. Louis also recommended going to Paris.

Once there, ride to the top of the Eiffel Tower and scan the entire 360 degree view. Look at the Pantheon. Gaze upon the Seine River, with the boats gliding up and down. Take in Notre Dame Cathedral, study the Louvre, the Paris Opera House, the Square of Louis the 14th and the whole panorama.

Louis L'Amour also recommended studying great music, poetry, art and architecture. He drove his point home when he described walking into the Louvre, with its abundance of magnificent art treasures. "If you take sex, passion and desire out of the Louvre," Louis used to say, "there would be nothing left. It will be an empty building."

Ideation techniques or any other attempts to tap into the creativity of the universe will be hollow if there is no passion. Sex, passion and desire could well be the difference between thinking out of the box and breaking out of the box! Try to include in the budget for things that produce "sex, passion and desire."

Make do with what you have

Thomas Edison strongly believed in making do with what was available in his quests to uncover creativity in the universe. He felt making do with the resources available is a powerful stimulant of creativity. Part of what made the United States an industrial and agricultural leader in the world is the ingenuity to be creative with existing resources.

Examples of individuals who took available resources and developed brilliant breakthrough inventions are numerous. In Korea, Mike's unusual sleeping bag environment was an example of making do with what was available. Edison had enormous breakthrough ideas.

Leonardo da Vinci's practice of taking notes and keeping a journal of observations (data collection) was a breakout idea. He also broke out with the idea to build models and prototypes. To study natural phenomenon the way it occurs is the essence of curiosity and the pathway to uncovering general principles.

Frank Lloyd Wright was a "breakout" architect. When he designed the beautiful house called Falling Waters at Bear Run, Pennsylvania, he didn't do the obvious. He was commissioned to design a home oriented to the waterfalls. The ordinary architect would have built a house with a view facing the waterfalls. Not Frank Lloyd Wright. His breakout idea was to build the house on top of the waterfall. He made the house part of the environment. The waterfalls cascade over and under the house and the sound is constant and soothing. There is even a waterfall shower—cold, but completely natural.

We had lunch one day with Tom Monohan, the founder of Domino's Pizza and a big fan of Frank Lloyd Wright. As we talked to Tom about our mutual admiration for Wright, Tom pointed out that Wright once said that a house should not be built *on* a hill, but rather should be *of* the hill. Thinking out of the box.

Another friend of ours, Robert Fiore, has spent a lifetime bringing fresh ideas to the people side of the gaming industry. He runs a large casino where he puts the people factor first in his operations. Bob is a man of the hill. He embodies the concept of becoming part of what he does. A good principle for each of us. The more detached we are from what we work on, the less opportunity our products or services have to become breakout ideas.

Walt Disney is almost too big a subject to tackle. His original ideas are legion. The team working on the film *Snow White and the Seven Dwarfs* asked Walt for advice on how to ensure the film would be truly outstanding. Walt's response was, "Better drawings." That idea would later lead to the establishment of the California Institute of the Arts. Walt brought in live animals and used live human figures to model for the animators. Thus, in the 1930s, Walt Disney Productions became a learning organization, dedicated to long-term education and development. Walt's simple concept of doing better animation than ever before was a breakout idea that called for thinking out of the box.

When he was doing the motion picture *Fantasia,* Walt decided to break out with better sound. "Fantasound" was born to produce the most dynamic reproduction possible for the orchestra under the direction of Leopold Stokowski. Fantasound was the first stereophonic sound in motion picture theaters.

The ideation techniques we've described to you in this chapter lead to original thinking and can lead to breakout thinking as well. These principles and methods will help you and your entire organization to do more than think out of the box. No matter how uncreative you think your team is, these techniques will help you break out of the box!

Jack Welch: Cooperation

The journey that led to our first meeting with the inimitable Jack Welch was like following the yellow brick road. In this case, the final destination was the Land of GE. Jack was the Wizard, pulling levers behind a curtain to create a new, innovative leadership style.

It all began when Len Vickers, Jack's assistant, approached Mike to ask him to make a presentation at GE's upcoming annual managers' meeting at Pinehurst Golf Resort.

Mike joked during his speech about how many wingtipped shoes there were in the audience and how wingtip thinking represents one of the biggest problems in American business. He told the audience that anyone wearing wingtips should take them off right away and have them bronzed like baby shoes.

Following the presentation, a GE executive approached the podium holding a pair of wingtip shoes he had just removed. The audience exploded in laughter as he held the shoes high in the air for everyone to see. Someone in the audience yelled, "Now that you've got them off, keep them off!" The man who yelled was Jack Welch.

Jack Welch, then vice chairman of GE, visited the Vance Creative Thinking Center to spend a day with us. He was joined by some of his team who were attempting to design a new light bulb. We had a work out with a truly exhilarating leader. He talked straight talk to his GE team, and they talked straight back to him. The atmosphere was not conducive to timidity or evasive politicking.

That's when Jack first told the group, "We have to weed out bureaucracies before they become jungles. Bureaucracies will eat you alive. Let's keep our organizational structure simple and let people take their own initiative. We want autonomy and entrepreneurship. We also want to be better than the best."

The personal touch

By the end of that productive day, Jack faced each member of the team one by one, shook their hands, looked directly into their souls, and said something intensely personal to each one, just as he had done to Mike when they first met. He made constructive suggestions and praised his people. He touched each one as he demonstrated a tremendous quality that stimulates creativity in others. He encouraged and built up others.

Personal contact with leaders causes inspiration, which stirs the creative spirit. Contact helps the leader to bond with his or her people, which is essential in transmitting vision. Personal contact is a best practice of highly creative people and an attribute of out-of-the-box thinkers. Before leaving, Jack looked at Mike and then around the Team Center and said, "Build one of these places for us." We built a Team Center at the GE locomotive division at Erie, Pennsylvania. We celebrated at the Pine Lake Trout Club in Ohio when the contract was signed.

This unique center was designed by our collaborative group. The GE project became an early model and prototype for business Team Centers, Group Rooms and Kitchens for the Mind, using work outs, boundaryless culture and the visual working method we call Displayed Thinking.

Thinking out of the Erie box

Think-out-of-the-box techniques were all operational at the Erie Team Center. Those methods and techniques were early precursors to new leadership methods. There have been many people who have taken undeserved credit for these leadership practices. But it was Jack Welch who first embraced them and put them into practice in his company.

The GE project was a seminal experience and a fresh approach to getting things accomplished in a manufacturing environment. The Team Center used Displayed Thinking, an indispensable part of the creative thinking process. The approach takes us beyond mere reengineering practices into reculturing the organization first with an entirely different set of values. Jack had the wisdom to combine method with his mission and vision.

Boundaryless and participatory environments are called different things—Creative Centers, The Pit, The Method Center, Kitchen for the Mind, etc. Regardless of the name, the function is essentially the same—to build a resource-rich setting in which people meet and work to create and to communicate with high visibility. Jack Welch described it best: "One room, one team, one coffee pot, one vision."

A solid leader

Jack is a firm believer in simplifying everything. He continues an ongoing crusade against rigidity, formality and bureaucracy. It was Jack Welch who encouraged the writing of this book. Jack's annual Christmas card always contains a personal challenge of some kind to keep wiping out bureaucracies.

We've been puzzled by Jack's reputation as a tough guy. After knowing him, we've learned that his image as heartless, caustic, irascible, even mean, is one-sided. There is also an unquestionable positive side to him. He is tough. He is not soft. But he is sensitive and deeply caring.

To us, Jack Welch represents sound leadership, especially in his willingness to take the heat in the course of maintaining a strong company. We can think of CEOs who are weak and wishy-washy in their resolve. As you might expect, many of them run their companies into the ground. If you see a company in shambles, you can bet it has wishy-washy leadership.

Jack Welch is the genuine article—nothing phony. We've talked to many executives who also recognize Jack's talents and abilities. But few of them are willing to pay the price Jack has been willing to pay, which has earned him respect and admiration. They need to read *The Wizard of Oz* again. Some of Jack Welch's best practices include:

- Simplified structures.
- Autonomy.
- Entrepreneurship.
- Work outs.
- Organizational innovation.
- Cultural transformation.
- Technical expertise.
- Straight talk.
- Open agenda.

CHAPTER 9

Inspiration: the missing link

"...one of the things we need around here is inspiration."
—E. Cardon Walker, Disney CEO

Inspired leadership is often the missing link in creative thinking in the business world. There are few courses on how to be an inspiring leader—and yet it is such a critical component of creative success. When leaders lack the ability to inspire, all of the other techniques, processes and methods add up to nothing.

It's far more beneficial for your bottom line and long-term success if you learn to be an inspirational leader. In fact, you should put everyone in your organization on the track to becoming an inspirational leader. Can you imagine what your organization could become if you have inspired people inspiring one another?

The alternative is not a promising picture. The weakest, or missing, link in companies we observe is the ability of leadership to inspire and motivate people. When we first started working with a Fortune 500 company, we heard an amazing story about its colorful chairman. While possibly apocryphal, it is nonetheless to-the-point. He reportedly said,

"I can't get my people to do what I want them to do because of the bureaucracies, and I'm the (expletive deleted) chairman!" We know many leaders who have felt this same frustration.

What we fail to realize is that in the transformational process, the challenge isn't getting people to do what we want them to do but to want the same things we want. The way we get people pulling for the same cause is to make them as much a part of the cause as possible. Better yet, make the cause as much a part of *them* as possible.

We described in earlier chapters how keeping people informed and involved in the creative process contributes to motivation and inspiration. But being involved and informed requires the additional component of inspiration in order to guarantee results and assure high creative performance. Leadership should follow through to make sure people are affected by their involvement. You can't just sit by and assume your people will be motivated and turned on.

We know of few organizational success stories that take place in the absence of inspiration. Organizations often have many of the qualities necessary for leadership but lack the inspirational leadership to take them over the top. Without inspirational leadership, what's going to keep the organization going when times get tough?

It's no wonder inspirational leadership is overlooked as an ingredient for organizational success. As we've become more and more consumed with the bottom line, the results are that pencil-pushing bottom-liners have been promoted into leadership positions. Men and women who have no clue how to involve, inform, inspire and motivate others are running too many organizations. Nobody's arguing the need to produce profits and impressive returns on shareholders' investments. But we know good bottom-line results are a byproduct of good top-line thinking. Watch the pencil-pushing bottom-liners joyfully count the money an inspired organization rakes in.

What goes up...

Some well-run companies have eventually declined when greed contaminates their cultures. Becoming obsessed with running lean and mean can lead to a sick and weak organization. There is an ever-present danger that a well-run organization can quickly become a poorly run organization. It can happen to anybody, and it can happen fast.

The common knee-jerk reaction is to downsize, reduce training and curtail enrichment programs. It's sometimes called reengineering, restructuring, rightsizing, you name it. Organizational development used to be a term that stood for developing people. Over the years, the term has come to stand for layoffs and outbound counseling. Step back for a moment and consider the message sent by downsizing and cutting training programs.

Especially when executives are paid big money for running their organizations, it's counterproductive to put people at the bottom of their priority list. How can leaders say they are dedicated to the growth and development of people if they slash anything related to the growth and development of people at the first sign of financial difficulty? How can leaders claim to believe in the team concept but spend more time in the ivory tower poring over financial reports?

Cutting staff size and training programs as the first alternative to bad financial news is a dead giveaway that the leader probably didn't understand the value of people to begin with. When policymakers really believe in the human factor, they invest more in people—not less—when times get tough, because it's the people who can change things. Corporate leaders should look at their own performance more objectively and not just blame those further down the organization. We should sell off a few buildings rather than just people.

Another knee-jerk reaction is often to build a new corporate head-quarters, redecorate or expand. But buildings in and of themselves have no dreams. They can't think up new products or services. They can't strategize or plot new courses. Buildings can't provide inspired leadership or build trust when trust and inspiration are what an organization needs most.

We've seen organizations put the squeeze on their people until they nearly suffocate them, and then cut back on their oxygen some more! Excessive controls and pressure for increased performance have the opposite of their intended effect. Leadership's time-honored and patented remedies—pressure and control—will eliminate the very initiative and creativity needed to get the results the pressure and control are intended to produce. If physicians practiced medicine the way some executives lead organizations, they would still be letting blood.

We know there are times when restructuring is necessary. The poor practices of poor leadership will invariably lead to top-heavy organizations, steeped in the bureaucracy that Jack Welch resists. When there are more people sitting on the bench than playing in the game, you have to question how competent the coach is. Good leadership practices don't lead to fat organizations. The real definition of lean and mean is highly functioning teams, engaged in creating better products and services.

There is a profound difference between downsizing and cleaning house. Replacing incompetent and noncontributing people is one thing, but downsizing may eliminate people who are more talented and capable than some of the people who initiate the cutbacks. Regretfully, many experts predict that downsizing in the United States has only begun. Despite everything we talk about and teach concerning sensible personnel practices, we need further work to find better alternatives for solving the problem. As long as leaders see downsizing as the only solution available to them, the people problems plaguing organizations will continue to be misunderstood.

The wrong message

At the same time some managers are eliminating people and pressuring employees for better performance, they're still awarding themselves big bonuses, remodeling their offices and buying new corporate jets. Those of us who wish to inspire others must be credible. If we don't have the ability or the desire to inspire others we will not be in leadership very long. However, we know CEOs who are thinking more long-range by being consistent and equitable in their treatment of people. Leadership is undergoing a massive transformation today.

When we talk about the inability or lack of desire to inspire people, we're talking about a big leadership vacuum that needs our attention. To be sure, it takes effort to be an inspirational leader, yet too few even try.

Thomas Edison said, "Genius is 1 percent inspiration and 99 percent perspiration." We agree. However, that one percent is the yeast that makes the bread rise.

A breakthrough bottom-liner

Roy O. Disney was a fantastic man who completely understood the importance of inspired leadership. Even though he headed the financial side of the company, he was also people-oriented. Roy was a consummate bottom-liner who appreciated the value of keeping people involved, informed and inspired. He could have taught a course on people skills for financial managers.

Roy was a good friend to Mike during his Disney career. Roy always found time to be available to Mike and others for training and development programs. Roy was a constant supporter of organizational development research projects. Roy spent hours talking with Mike about the Disney Way and the company philosophy before he felt comfortable enough for Mike to teach it.

Like his brother Walt, Roy was a big supporter of the family and getting spouses involved. He hosted a luncheon or dinner with every development group that came through Mike's program. After Walt's death, Roy invited spouses to the Coral Room meals during which he explained the company's future. There are few board chairmen who would be so up-front and honest with their people.

Especially in the early days at Disney, management took time with people, invested the necessary capital to get the job done right, got into the trenches whenever necessary and didn't practice elitism. The legacy for Disney leaders was built on a participatory model. The original OD paradigm at Disney paved the way for future Disney leaders to understand the rich culture and traditions upon which they could build. The great financial success of the Disney organization today rests firmly on the solid foundation laid by the founders.

Roy Disney didn't make a big deal out of inspiration. He wasn't a grandstander. He was just a good, decent, sincere and truly smart—but often underrated—man from Kansas. Those who dubbed him the "other Disney brother" didn't know the score. Roy's contributions to the Disney success story were significant. As with many quiet but effective leaders, Roy was understated. People sometimes misjudged his quiet resolve as a lack of power or influence. He lacked neither. The worst rub of all was that such people didn't avail themselves of Roy's sage advice.

Roy was talking to Mike and a group of executives in the Disney board of directors room, which was next to his office, when Merrill Dean, a fast-rising Disney executive, asked Roy what the secret was to the company's incredible success. Roy said, "It's no secret. We've always tried to manage by our values because, when you know what your values are, decision-making is easier. We believe that top-line thinking is the cause which produces good bottom-line results, or the effect.

"You've got to have your values in synch with your goals; then people are self-motivated. They don't require a shot in the arm or motivational hype, although it doesn't hurt to perk things up once in awhile.

"Most people have ability. You've got to encourage them by setting lofty standards and then help them master their skills. This is why we put so much emphasis on training and education."

This was the conversation that inspired Mike to begin developing the "Management By Values" leadership course for the Disney University. Years later, A.C. (Mike) Markkula, chairman of Apple Computer, prodded Mike to take the concept further and create the current "Management By Values" audiocassette program. Markkula continued to insist that Mike's ideas be synthesized into a concise statement everyone could understand and apply. This led to the formation of the "New Leadership Paradigm" concept, inspired by Roy Disney:

"Leadership is the ability to establish standards and manage a creative climate where people are self-motivated toward the mastery of long-term constructive goals in a participatory environment of mutual respect compatible with personal values."

This definition of leadership is in wide circulation today and is the core of both the "Management By Values" and the "New Leadership Paradigm" audiocassette programs. Roy Disney's influence on Mike's career and beliefs is obvious. Roy had a creative side that was often masked by his low-key personality.

Roy asked Mike an interesting question one day during the construction phase of Walt Disney World. They were standing on Main Street in the Magic Kingdom when Roy asked what the park guests would do during the regular midday thunderstorms common to central Florida.

Mike recommended perhaps a "rain parade" would do. "What's a rain parade?" Roy asked. Mike replied that he wasn't sure himself, but it sounded good off the top of his head. That same evening, after dinner, Roy, Mike and Bob Jani, director of the entertainment division, were sitting around the swimming pool at the Hilton Inn, which Disney had taken over for training purposes prior to the opening of Disney World. Roy asked Mike if he'd told Bob about the rain parade idea yet. Mike hadn't. Roy said he'd been thinking about the idea since Mike first mentioned it and thought they could possibly have some sort of parade out on Bay Lake and bring it right up onto Main Street as a finale.

Bob's interest was aroused and he mentioned that he'd already been thinking about doing some type of show on the lake with Handel's "Water Music," lights and an electronic synthesizer. The small group continued talking about the idea for a long time, enjoying the balmy Florida evening, drinking and nibbling on a bowl of chips. Roy passed out cigars as other Disney people stopped by the pool to chat with him and have a drink.

Bob Jani kept after the idea with his creative staff back in California and eventually developed the nightly electronic display on Bay Lake and the world-famous Main Street Electric Parade—both of which are Disney classics.

Incidentally, Bob Jani later left the Disney organization and reopened Radio City Music Hall in New York City. We visited Bob often in New York. On one such occasion, we were having dinner in the Oak Room of the Plaza Hotel at the same time Buckminster Fuller was dining there. The topic of conversation turned to Roy Disney and Mike's most memorable experience with him.

Yippie day at Disneyland

The best way to teach the principle of inspirational leadership is by example and modeling. Roy was just such a role model for all leaders who want to inspire their people. As we mentioned, Roy wasn't a grandstander. However, he stood several feet taller than his 5'4" frame when he was presented with a challenge. Yippie Day at Disneyland, in Anaheim, California, was a terrible day on one hand and a triumphant one on the other.

The turbulent days of the late 1960s and the Vietnam War were tearing the American people apart. There were protests against every form of social injustice—real or imagined. The Yippies were an intensely focused and sometimes violent offshoot of the otherwise peaceful Hippie movement. Tensions were running high between dissenters and authorities everywhere, and Anaheim was no exception. There was a patriotic stage production running at Disneyland. This was an irresistible target for the Yippies, who were in a most unpatriotic mood.

Disney was a ripe target for antiestablishment protest because of the obvious publicity such protests would generate. Word came to the company that the Yippies were planning a violent uprising at Disneyland, including fires and disruption of operations and attractions. The threat was taken seriously, in part because of the recent firebombing of a Bank of America branch in northern California. The same group claimed responsibility. Disneyland management elected not to cave in to the threat and close the park on the appointed day. However, preparations were carefully made to handle any problems that might arise. Roy was at the park with other Disney executives on the announced day of the protest.

Hundreds of Yippies showed up as expected. They were granted admission to the park and proceeded to cause a wide variety of problems throughout the day. Mike was at Roy's right hand throughout the ordeal. The disruptions finally began to get out of hand, and it was decided to close the park for the safety of the guests. Riot police, dressed in ominous black uniforms with helmets, batons and shields, lined both sides of Main Street from Town Square to Carnation Plaza and the Plaza Inn as the guests filed out.

The scene was frighteningly out of place at Disneyland, an environment Walt Disney created as an escape from the realities of life beyond the front gate. The police in riot gear were in stark contrast to the backdrop of the "happiest place on earth." A fistfight broke out between Dick Nunis, the head of Disneyland, and one of the scraggly Yippies. It was no contest, and Dick personally carried the instigator out of the park amidst the cheers of the crowd.

Card Walker walked over to Roy after the skirmish and said, "I'm sorry, Roy. We're doing our best to handle this." Roy let him know that he understood their predicament. Characteristic of great leadership, Roy pondered the day's events deeply and questioned his own role. He said, "The hostility being displayed here today rests squarely on the shoulders of my generation. We have not been responsive to the wants and needs of young people. There are social injustices we have just plain ignored for years.

"My generation has often been closed minded to their needs and wants. As a result, we have let the family nearly disintegrate since World War II. We've got to work on these issues right away. Next time they might burn the whole place down. We must educate better, train harder, create more opportunity, help youth get a start in life and get our house in order."

Roy and Mike then walked to the front gate area where ousted Yippies were throwing bottles over the fence. It was a chaotic scene. A young reporter for the Associated Press approached Roy and said, "Mr. Disney, shouldn't you get out of here? You could get hurt." Roy replied, "Young man, don't you think the risk is worth it for me to be here?" The reporter got it. "Yes, sir," he said knowingly. Roy was involved, and his people were inspired. Great pains had been taken to make sure everyone in the organization had been informed and they worked as a team with soaring spirits and morale.

Roy Disney, at 5'4", was a towering inspiration on that dangerous day at Disneyland. He was in the trenches with his people, and so were Card Walker and Dick Nunis. How many top executives today walk into the line of fire with their people and tough it out? On the day when Disneyland guests and Disneyland employees needed leadership the most, their leaders weren't back at headquarters being briefed on the situation. They weren't fishing for marlin off the coast of Mexico. They weren't off buying art. They were there!

Disney leadership, from the top on down, was standing nose-to-nose with the crisis and shoulder-to-shoulder with their people. There was no absentee management on Yippie Day at Disneyland. Management's willingness to courageously confront the problem was inspirational. Executives today who are willing to stand amidst the smashing bottles without flinching, the way Roy Disney did, motivate their people by example and produce organizations that perform beyond their shareholders' wildest imaginations. We set examples like Roy Disney in front of you to demonstrate that the concepts and principles we admire are real. Inspirational leadership has to be flesh and blood.

Our profiles of great leadership come from experience. If we expect people to think out of the box, inspirational leadership will be the yeast to make spirits rise.

Walt Disney: Creativity

The creative person is one who harnesses the creative process in pursuing the greatest art form of them all—meaningful living. The creative person achieves personal fulfillment through participation in life's most rewarding activity—productive thought. The creative person enjoys the beauty and warmth of the rising sun, envisions the potential of the human race, hurls artificial orbiting stars into the sky, cares for little children, builds bird sanctuaries by the water's edge and contemplates what is out there in the darkness beyond the night.

Walt Disney exemplified the creative person in every way. There are few people in history who match Walt's creativity, both artistically and commercially. Like anyone who makes a profound influence on his or her culture, he had his detractors, too. But no one can argue that he didn't bring wholesome entertainment based on positive values to millions of people around the world.

Walt was creativity personified. He was a multitalented human being with a timeless devotion to excellence and a penchant for good taste. He was an artist, filmmaker and inventor. Undoubtedly, his most spectacular achievement and gift to the world was Disneyland and Walt Disney World—they are without equal.

"If you want to get rich, find something no one wants anymore and make it valuable by what you do to it."

185

Walt Disney more than said that, he did it. He completely reconstructed an old industry that was tired, worn-out and had developed a terrible reputation. Amusement parks, fairs and carnivals were known for dishonesty, drug dealing and poor child labor practices. Walt made the industry respectable through his own devotion to values and high standards and an unrelenting quest for excellence in everything he did. He invented the theme park by raising the amusement park to an entirely new level.

Theme parks have become a major leisure-time business around the world with a promising future. Children and adults who enjoy these places owe a debt of gratitude to Walt Disney for his vision of Disneyland and the tenacity required to make the dream a reality. Disneyland has brought happiness and joy to many millions of guests since the park opened on July 17, 1955. The standards at work at Disneyland have raised the bar for other operations. Visitors to Disney properties constantly express their high regard for Disney's overall quality, presentation and employee performance.

It's not uncommon for entrepreneurs to say, "Let's do it as well as Disney." This enviable reputation, built on a foundation of quality standards and high values, is the source of Disney's gold mine. Disney's next generation of policymakers must guard their legacy like Fort Knox.

Who's the SOB?

The Disney organization is known for combining a hard-nosed standard with a soft-hearted approach toward employee and guest relations. A Walt Disney World executive used to say, "There is only one SOB allowed around here, and it's me. The rest of you are nice guys." This simplistic leadership technique, combined with magnificent training, puts the magic in the Magic Kingdom.

We've heard countless stories about Walt Disney at organizational development dinners from old hands who had been at Disney since the beginning. These are apocryphal tales, even though there were numerous versions of the same story. We hope our renditions are reasonably close to the actual circumstances.

Pass on the figs

Mel Melton, president of a Disney subsidiary, told of a humorous episode that took place as Walt was traveling with a group of his executives.

The six executives were assembled for breakfast in a hotel dining room, waiting for Walt to join them.

They decided to delay placing their orders until he arrived. He eventually walked into the restaurant, sat down and asked what they were waiting for and why they hadn't ordered. One of them told Walt that they had been waiting for him to arrive.

The waitress asked Walt what he wanted to start with and he ordered fresh figs. She asked the six other men at the table what they wanted to start with and they all ordered figs. As the story goes, Walt leaped to his feet and exclaimed, "I hate figs! I hate people who like figs. I hate people who copy other people who copy other people who say they like figs. In fact, I hate you guys, too."

He walked out on them and flew back to California on the company plane, leaving his surprised executives stunned. This story has long been legend among Disneyites as an example of Walt's loathing for people who copy other people instead of exercising their own creativity. A word to the wise: Create rather than copy.

A big heart

Bob Jackson, Walt's press representative, related an incident revealing Walt's compassion for anyone or anything suffering or hurting. The publicity department at the studio received a letter addressed to Walt Disney from a family in the Midwest whose 10-year-old son was dying of cancer. They were deeply concerned because the boy's one wish was to visit Disneyland when it was completed.

Walt invited the family to visit the unfinished park and paid for their entire trip. On the appointed day, Walt requested that the Disneyland train be placed on the tracks so he could take the boy for a ride. He was told this would be impossible because of production schedules. Walt accepted no excuses and his will was done.

Bob told us how inspiring it was to see Walt carrying the boy up the steps of the train station in town square. With the boy in his lap, he drove the train around the perimeter of the park. Construction workers throughout the property paused as Walt and the boy passed them on the train. Maybe they wanted to capture a little of that human kindness for themselves. This was Walt Disney at his best. A big heart is often a characteristic of highly creative people.

Two-fisted Walt

Don't misjudge Walt Disney by the last story. He wasn't maudlin in any way or mushy in his responses. He was authentic with occasional acerbic and sarcastic remarks. We gathered suitable quotes about Walt to use in our Disney Way course at Disney University. Mike Bagnell, Randy Bright, Pam Canel, Van France, Lou Johnson, John McCauley, Dick Milano, Betty Seeber, Sausha Sherban, John Que, Bob Warren and Bob White all worked with Mike at Disney "U" to assemble what would be titled "Quotes, Recollections and Vast Achievements of Walt Disney."

"The mythmaker is a primitive. He molds his fantasies out of primordial impulses that are common to all men. In an age of reality, he is a rarity, for he celebrates an innocence that does not mix well with the times. Walt Disney was such a man, molding myths and spinning fantasies in which innocence always reigned. Literally billions of people responded...and they lavished their gratitude on him. Soldiers carried the cartoon-figure emblems of his creations on their uniforms and their war planes. Kings and dictators saw them as symbols of some mysterious quality of the American character. David Tom, the great British cartoonist, called Disney 'the most significant figure in graphic arts since Leonardo.' Harvard and Yale gave him honorary degrees in the same year (1938); on his shelves are more than 900 citations; including an unprecedented 31 Academy Awards."

—*Time* magazine, December 23, 1966

"The word fabulous, as applied to Walt Disney, is an understatement. He was a genius, an originator, a creative artist of amazing versatility, a master organizer and administrator, a producer of perfection, a daring adventurer."

—*Columbus Citizen Journal*

"I couldn't realize what my father did for a living until I was six. Then a playmate at school told me. That night when Father came home he flopped down into his easy chair. I approached him with awe. 'Are you Walt Disney?' I asked. He didn't look famous to me."

—Diane Disney Miller, *The Story of Walt Disney*

"No eulogy will be read or monument built to equal the memorial Walt Disney has left in the hearts and minds and imaginations of the world's people."

—Richard D. Zanuck, motion picture producer

"Everyone who knew him agreed Disney loved to work, although there may have been differences in the view of how he achieved his results. He has young people in many key spots, but he himself never lost touch with any project from its start, in the opinion of some. Another viewpoint had been of Walt moving from project to project in the company private plane, impatient in dealing with actors, writers and employees, and always tight-fisted. These people even say he was often grumpy, unintentionally, although other associates denied this, but concede he was a perfectionist. It was also observed that for all his heavy load of work, he still took time out to check light bulbs burned out and see to it there were no dirty washrooms."

—*Los Angeles Herald Examiner*

"Under the breezy surface this man evidently had thought a good deal about grimness. But only the very serious can provide the sense of fantasy which, in the guise of pleasant madness, helps the world keep its sanity."

—Yousuf Karsh

What Walt said:

"I can never stand still. I must explore and experiment.
I am never satisfied with my work.
I resent the limitations of my own imaginations."

"Fantasies and reality often overlap."

"My greatest reward is that I've been able to build
this wonderful organization, have good health and to
have the public appreciate and accept what I've done."

"We keep moving forward, opening new doors
and doing new things, because we're curious."

"Disneyland will continue to grow, to add new things,
as long as there is imagination left in the world."

"You're only as good as your next picture."

"...I see the City of Tomorrow in Florida as a place
where people can actually live, and work, and feel like
they do when they visit Disneyland for the first time."

"Deeds rather than words express my concept
of the part religion should play in everyday life.
I have watched constantly that in our work the highest
moral and spiritual standards are upheld."

"Never get bored or cynical. Yesterday is a thing of the past."

"You may not realize it when it happens, but a kick
in the teeth might be the best thing in the world for you."

"Man needs a new set of problems to pull
his mind away from the old ones."

"All you've got to do is own up to your ignorance honestly, and
you'll find people who are eager to fill your head with information."

The man...the mystery

In spite of these enlightening quotes, the real Walt Disney remains an enigma, even to many people who worked with him for 30 years or more. Everyone puts a slight twist on a changing kaleidoscopic picture of the man. Mike had more than 200 dinners and lunches with his business associates during his tenure at The Walt Disney Company. They spent countless hours of open, constructive conversation about Walt with those closest to him for many years.

For Mike, one personal experience highlighted Walt's unusual creativity. Walt had a unique way of looking at ordinary things most people merely passed by unnoticed. It was a morning just a few months before his death. His behavior was different from anything Mike had experienced before or that other people closer to him had ever mentioned. It was 1965. A gentle rain fell as Mike walked from his car into the studio that morning. Walt drove his Mercedes Coupe through the front gate, waving as he pulled into his parking space.

Mike waited for him, chatting with a guard named Bill. Walt slowly approached the two men and asked, "How do you guys like the fresh rain this morning?" He seemed to be in a very good mood, and they walked through the studio grounds toward the animation building, where their offices were located on the third floor. It was an experience similar to the day Walt walked with Mike and Emmett McGaughey down Mickey Mouse Drive when Walt wished Mike luck with whatever he did in life. As they walked, Walt took an interest in a blooming oleander bush near the sidewalk by the studio theater. He stopped to examine it.

"Look at the tiny water bubble sitting on this leaf. I wonder how that bubble appears to the leaf? It probably looks like a giant dome. You know, we should have a bubble restaurant floating around on a huge leaf on Bay Lake in Florida. We could call it the Floating Bubble Restaurant. Did you ever think about how many bubbles there are in an entire ocean? Think of the amount of life and creativity there is in an entire ocean."[1]

---

[1]Later, a Disney artist drew us a picture of a floating bubble restaurant for an OD project.

They continued walking and Mike remarked, "People say that every snowflake has a different design. Think of how much creativity there is in a backyard full of snow." Walt interrupted, "Yes, creativity is everywhere. You can't get away from it. The important thing is to put your two cents' worth into something and make a difference."

Walt paused again in front of a window with wooden frames to observe the water trickling down the glass to form a small pool on the ground below. He reflected again:

"Do you remember when you were a little boy and it would be raining hard outside? Do you remember how good it felt to be warm and cozy inside your house with a warm fire burning in the fireplace? Do you remember how secure it made you feel? Do you remember the smell? These are exciting things to remember.

"Do you remember seeing youngsters outside your house scurrying along in the rain, splashing and jumping in the puddles and wondering what it must be like to be big? Did you ever dream about what you were going to do when you got big? Did you ever get the urge to grow up and do everything fast? Like me, I'm impatient to get on with it."

By then they had reached the steps of the animation building. Walt stopped again and made another comment that Mike will take with him to the grave. "Do you want to know something more exciting than what we've been talking about?" Before Mike could answer, Walt rushed on.

"It's to be an adult like we are now and look back through the window of memory, remembering the time when we were little children, but it's even more exciting to know that we became the kind of people we dreamed about as children. Do you know what that's called?"

Mike shook his head to the rhetorical question.

"Fulfillment! This is called fulfillment. It's what every person hopes life will be like for them. I hope you have that kind of feeling in your life, Mike. I hope you become what you dreamed you could be when you were a little boy."

This was Walt at his purest and best. This was the Walt the world came to love and admire. He wasn't a false image. He was real. There was no enigma in that moment. Mike never had such a private and intimate walk with Walt before that day, and he never would again. Creativity can be awakened by a slow walk in gently falling rain. Out-of-the-box thinkers create rather than copy.

Some of Walt Disney's best practices include:

- Gag sessions.
- Powwows.
- Storyboards.
- Technology.
- Fantasy.
- Long-range planning.
- Attention to detail.
- Originality.
- Innovation.
- Vision.
- Involvement.

The urge to create

The place: Eiffel Tower—Paris, France.

The people: Diane Deacon, Mike Vance and Mike's daughter,
Vanessa Vance.

The product: people's creations.

We anxiously walked through the entrance gate to the Eiffel Tower,
noting the neon number flashing on the electronic admission counter
which indicated that 159,750,557 people had gone through the turnstile
before us. The three of us made it 159,750,560. Thomas Edison had
been one of those numbers a long time ago. We recommend that each
of you get involved with us by adding your number to the count.
Concorde to Paris.

We speculated whether the designer, French engineer Gustov Eiffel,
if he were here today, would believe so many people had reveled at his
grand creation.

We entered the inclined elevator; 984 feet later we stepped out to a
view of Paris that Napoleon or Marie Antoinette never enjoyed. Vanessa
Vance exclaimed, "Oh, my God!" as we stood together on the observation platform surveying the incomparable panorama of one of the
world's most spectacular cities. With one sweep of our eyes, we
embraced the celebrated legends and landmarks that have drawn so

many people like us from around the world to experience a celebration of humankind's urge to create.

There's no greater inspiration than to stand atop the Eiffel Tower at twilight on a balmy summer evening with someone you love. The picturesque boats and lighted bridges of the River Seine (there's Cary Grant and Audrey Hepburn), Notre Dame Cathedral, the Louvre, the Basilica of the Sacred Heart, Montmartre, the Paris Opera House and the Majestic Pantheon were laid out before us.

Leonardo da Vinci, Dali, Joan of Arc, Napoleon, Rembrandt, Rubens, Venus de Milo, and even I.M. Pei[1] in his glass pyramid are out there. The ultimate view, we thought; heaven was surely close by. The Mona Lisa should be moved from her ensconced place in the Louvre to the Eiffel Tower for a better view of the city.

The consequences of man's urge to create were demonstrated among the streets and boulevards far below us. And yet, from this height, we could feel the urge throbbing in the Parisian *mise-en-scène* until it ignited our personal hunger for creative fulfillment. It was clear to us why Paris has been called a demanding mistress by writers and poets. Artists are driven to paint Notre Dame over and over because of its architectural splendor, while in stark contrast girls from the Moulin Rouge pull up their skirts dancing the can-can.

We could hear Louis L'Amour reminding us that sex, passion and desire enflame creativity. These are the themes, either directly or indirectly, which inspire every sculptor, every painter, every poet, every composer, every author and every lover.

This compelling urge to create was never personified better than in the man who took an old dirty swamp in the middle of Florida and transformed it with his vision into a secular mecca visited by possibly more people than any other place in the world. He took a business with a sullied reputation—the amusement park, noted for drug dealing, cheating and child labor abuse—and made it into a masterpiece of imagination that served and cared for people.

---

[1]I.M. Pei (Ieoh Ming), the famous Chinese-American architect, designed the glass pyramid at the Louvre. Pei is considered by many to be the greatest living architect.

Walter Elias Disney—his number really scored high on the big counter of those who have thought out of the box.

Then there is Admiral Joe Fowler, who built ships in World War II and was in charge of the construction of Disneyland and the construction startup of Walt Disney World. He was the can-do admiral. He never questioned, "Can we? Do we have the know-how? Do we have the resources? Do we have the time?" Joe asked, "When? When do you want it done? When do you need it?"

The fundamental attitude for thinking out of the box is the "when" attitude. For example, AT&T had divestiture a number of years ago, which resulted in a series of meetings across the country to prepare for enormous change. AT&T vice presidents and senior managers were gathered to discuss plans for the court-ordered breakup. Mike was invited to address each of these sessions, which consisted of several hundred executives.

Those who were planning the meetings knew Mike's philosophy of the "when" attitude and had heard him talk about Admiral Joe Fowler. Because they were changing their basic organization, they needed a new formula for building an entrepreneurial culture.

They would be competing in a way they had never competed in the past. It was a challenge. They prepared an impressive booklet of heavy-coated stock with tissue paper dividers to give each attendee as a momento of the event.

Embossed in gold leaf on dark brown leather was the word *When,* followed by the two provocative questions below:

If not me, who?
If not now, when?

The room at the top of the tower

There's a small room at the top of the Eiffel Tower in Paris, where a lifelike mannequin of Thomas Edison at work sits at a telegraph key. He is tapping out a message on the keypad as Gustov Eiffel watches him closely. We conjectured as to what message he might be sending way up there in the tower.

He was probably tapping the first words he reportedly shouted into his newly invented phonograph machine—"Hello, hello, hello out there. Create something for us."

Think out of the box.

Create something for us!

When? Now!

For further information on Mike Vance's and Diane Deacon's speaking programs, seminars, recorded training courses, consulting, etc., contact:

The Creative Thinking Association of America
16600 Sprague Road
Suite #120
Cleveland, Ohio 44130
216-243-5576
800-535-0030

■ GLOSSARY ■

Brain showers: Water figuratively washes away mind clutter.

Briefing Board: Visual method for before/during/after-the-fact controls.

Charrette: An intensive work out on a project using creative thinking techniques.

Creative Thinking Technique System: Tool for operationalizing creative thinking.

Defer status: Status given to an issue when it is deliberately put aside to be dealt with later.

Displayed Thinking: A method of visualizing concepts, ideas and facts used in planning, creating and working.

Dymaxion map: Buckminster Fuller's map correcting the distortions of the equator.

Fantasound: Sound designed for the motion picture *Fantasia* with stereophonic qualities.

Ideation techniques: Methods used to generate ideas.

Image-ination: Forming images in context of creative thought.

Kitchen for the Mind: A room filled with creativity-stimulating objects and decor; a Team Center for the home.

Law of Causality (Socrates): Behind every effect there is a cause.

Law of Identity (Aristotle): Something is what it is.

MICORBS: Mnemonic for remembering the seven ways to think out of the box.

Mind boggling: A free flow of ideas intended to blow your mind out of the box; a wild, unrestrained form of brainstorming.

Mind quake: Buckminster Fuller's term for explosive growth of information and knowledge taking place at any time.

New leadership paradigm: Mike's model of new leadership traits.

Nine-dot exercise: Exercise to demonstrate creative thinking.

Organizational development: Term coined by Card Walker to describe the cultural training of Disney employees in Florida.

Phantom team: Team created in one's mind by past experiences.

Psychosclerosis: Hardening of the mind.

Sand traps: Ideas that box people in.

Sensanation: Simultaneously thinking in all five senses.

Sorting: Placing index cards in the Displayed Thinking process under the appropriate subject.

Syllogism: Form of reasoning where conclusion is reached from two statements.

Tabula rasa: Clean slate.

Team Center: Resource-rich environment to serve as a gathering place for teams and individuals.

■ INDEX ■

A

Adler, Dr. Mortimer, 57, 143

American Institute of
  Architects, 83

Apple Computer, 7, 9-11, 43, 64,
  88-90, 152-3, 180

Apple Values, 87, 90, 153

Aristotle, 142-3, 149, 153,
  204, 143

Artifacts, 94

Art of friendship, 28-29

Associate with realistic
  people, 144

AT&T, 64, 84, 152, 197

Avon, 51

B

Bailey, Grace, 55

Barnum, P.T., 54

Beethoven, Ludwig von, 47

Best-kept secrets, 29, 114-115

Best practices, 34, 39, 62, 81, 94,
  115, 117, 124, 140, 153, 173, 193

Big decision, the, 121

Big heart, a, 187

Blue Bayou Restaurant, 36, 41

Body speak, 42-43

Brain showers, 56-58, 203

Brainstorming, 21, 158-160,
  162-164, 204

Brandt, Kent, 92

Breaks, new, 134-135

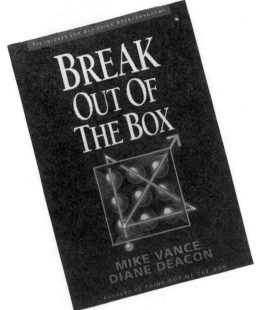